HOW DOES
THE BIBLE
SHAPE
MY FAITH?

HOW DOES THE BIBLE SHAPE MY FAITH?

*A Study of Biblical Interpretation
and Faith Development*

FaithQuestions SERIES

Ted Leach

ABINGDON PRESS
NASHVILLE

HOW DOES THE BIBLE SHAPE MY FAITH?
A Study of Biblical Interpretation and Faith Development

Copyright © 2006 by Abingdon Press

This book is printed on acid-free, elemental chlorine-free paper.

ISBN: 0-687-49739-6

06 07 08 09 10 11 12 13 14 15—10 9 8 7 6 5 4 3 2 1

MANUFACTURED IN THE UNITED STATES OF AMERICA

CONTENTS

HOW TO USE
How Does the Bible Shape My Faith?
A Study of Biblical Interpretation and Faith Development

How Does the Bible Shape My Faith? A Study of Biblical Interpretation and Faith Development invites participants to explore key questions about the many different ways that people of faith interpret the Bible in order to grow in their faith. Various interpretations of the Bible inform and enrich the daily practice of Christian faith. In each case, the Bible functions as the primary resource for faith development. The book is designed for use in any of three settings: (1) adult Sunday school, (2) weekday adult groups, and (3) retreat settings. It can also provide a meaningful resource for private study and reflection. You will find endnotes to direct you to other resources that will enrich your learning.

Sunday School: How Does the Bible Shape My Faith? may be used on Sunday mornings as a short-term, seven-week study. Sunday morning groups generally last 45 to 60 minutes. If your group would like to go into greater depth, you can divide the chapters and do the study for longer than seven weeks.

Weekday Study: If you use How Does the Bible Shape My Faith? in a weekday study, we recommend 90-minute sessions. Participants should prepare ahead by reading the content of the chapter and choosing one activity for deeper reflection and study. A group leader may wish to assign these activities.

Retreat Study: You may wish to use How Does the Bible Shape My Faith? in a more intense study like a weekend retreat. Distribute the books at least two weeks in advance. Locate and provide additional media resources and reference materials, such as Bible dictionaries and commentaries. Tell participants to read How Does the Bible Shape My Faith? before the retreat begins. Begin on Friday with an evening meal or refreshments followed by gathering time and worship. Discuss the Introduction and Chapter 1. Cover Chapters 2, 3, 4, and 5 on Saturday and Chapters 6 and 7 on Sunday. Develop a schedule that includes time for breaks, for meals, and for personal reflection of various topics in the chapters. End the retreat with closing worship on Sunday afternoon.

Leader/Learner Helps

Leader/learner helps are located in boxes near the relevant main text. They include a variety of discussion and reflection activities. Include both the Gathering and Closing worship activities in each session of your study, and choose from among the other leader/learner helps to fit the time frame you have chosen for your group.

The activities in the leader/learner helps meet the needs of a variety of personalities and ways of learning. They are designed to stimulate both solitary reflection and group discussion. An interactive and informal environment will foster a dynamic interchange of ideas and demonstrate the value of diverse perspectives. While the readings may be done in the group, reading outside of the session will enrich individual reflection and group discussion.

The Role of the Group Leader

A group leader facilitates gathering and closing worship, organizes the group for each session, monitors the use of time so that adequate attention is given to all major points of the chapter, and encourages an atmosphere of mutual respect and Christian caring. The leader should participate fully in the study as both learner and leader. The same person may lead all the sessions, or each session may have a different leader.

INTRODUCTION

The Bible

This is a study about some of the questions we bring to the Bible. A basic question to get us started is this: "What is the Bible?" The answer may seem obvious, but it's a good question. The word *bible* means "book," and this Book is shared by several faith groups. The word *Bible* may refer to the Hebrew Bible used today in Jewish synagogues, to the Old and New Testaments used in Protestant churches, or to the Bible used in Roman Catholic or Eastern Orthodox churches, which includes the Old and New Testaments as well as some additional writings.

For Jews

Jewish people use the word *Bible* to refer to the Hebrew Bible, a collection of writings recorded originally in the Hebrew language. Protestants know these writings as the "Old Testament."

For Protestants

The content of the Hebrew Bible is basically the same as the Old Testament used by Protestant Christians, though the books are arranged in a slightly different order.

For Roman Catholics and Eastern Orthodox Christians

Roman Catholic and Eastern Orthodox Christians include additional Jewish writings that were written originally in the Greek language not long before the time of Jesus. These writings are sometimes called "deuterocanonical writings" and are also known as the Apocrypha.

For Muslims

In today's world, it is vital for us to be aware that Islam, founded six centuries after Jesus, has monotheistic roots in the Bible. Muhammad, the founder of Islam, had some exposure to the Bible, to Judaism, and to Christianity. The Koran, a collection of Muhammad's recitations, contains references to the Bible and to some Christian stories not included in the Bible. Abraham is venerated by Jews, Christians, and Muslims alike.

The Importance of Questions

Good questions are essential in the learning process. Honest questions build relationships. Respectful questions create community. Healthy questions provide an atmosphere for engagement. Heartfelt questions that express both intellect and emotion form the essence of prayer.

What questions do you bring to the Bible? Occasionally someone will tell me that he or she has for a long time carried a particular question about the Bible but has been too embarrassed to ask the question in a group setting. Somewhere along the way, we may have been taught that it is not good, faithful, or reverent to ask serious questions about the Bible. This resistance to questions certainly did not come from the Bible! Within its pages we find searing, honest questioning arising between God and the people of faith.

One of the most poignant stories in the Bible is the conversation between Job and God in Job 38:1–42:6. The Book of Job is itself a question, or a plea for hearing, about why bad things happen to good people. The climax comes when God responds to Job's questions by saying, "*I will question you, and you shall declare to me*" (38:3, italics added). At first glance, this may seem like an end to the dialogue, as if God is saying, "Shut up and listen!" However, it is really an indication of the depth of intimacy, the radical honesty, and the probing mutuality going on in this back-and-forth questioning between God and Job.

If God didn't love Job (or us) so much, God wouldn't bother to ask such profound questions. A reading of Job 38–42 may seem to discourage questions of the Creator of the universe, but perhaps the point is that our questions to God should be good, honest, respectful, healthy, and heart-felt. God responds to Job with equal honesty: "Where were *you* when I laid the foundation for the earth?" (38:4, italics added). God, in a sense, puts Job *in his place*, but this "place" is an intimate, face-to-face encounter with the Almighty.

God cares enough about us to ask us deep questions about our attitudes and our practices. Do we care enough about God to ask our deepest questions? Leander Keck wrote a book years ago called *Taking the Bible Seriously*. Keck, who has the heart of a rabbi/teacher, understands that the best way to read the Bible is to *wrestle* with it, thus allowing the Bible to become what God intended it to be—a tool for honest dialogue.

Encountering God Through Questions

My prayer for this study is that we will bring our deepest and most honest questions to God and, in turn, hear whatever questions God has for us. This is true encounter, akin to what once happened when a lawyer asked Jesus a question: "Teacher, what must I do to inherit eternal life?" Jesus answered a good question with another question, asking, "What is written in the law?" The lawyer replied, "You shall love the Lord your God with all your heart, and with all your soul, and with all your strength, and with all your mind; and your neighbor as yourself." Jesus then said, "You have given the right answer; do this, and you will live" (Luke 10:25-28).

Each of our seven sessions will address a particular question about the Bible. My goal is to bring honest scholarship to your reading experience without being academic, abstract, or theoretical. My prayer is that these sessions will help you find simple and practical guidance from the Bible for living your daily life in our challenging and complex world.

Ted Leach

CHAPTER 1
WHO WROTE THE BIBLE?

Focus: The chapter explores how God inspires our faith development through those who collected, wrote, and edited the Bible.

Gathering

Greet one another. Write the question "Who wrote the Bible?" on a large sheet of newsprint or white paper. Tape this to a wall or other easily accessible location. Write responses to the question on the newsprint. Review the written responses with others in the group.

Pray the following prayer together: Loving and guiding God, we thank you for the Bible. We pray for your guidance as we explore how its writings teach us about you, about your will for us, and about who we can be as your people. In Christ we pray. Amen.

Inspired by God

Who wrote the Bible? If we ask that question to a group of kindergarten children in Sunday school, the likely answer would be, "God." While this may seem too simple, it reflects the church's belief that God is the creative force, the inspiration, behind Scripture.

The writer of First Timothy had in mind the Hebrew Bible, the Christian Old Testament, in saying, "All Scripture is God-breathed and is useful for teaching, rebuking, correcting and training in righteousness, so that all God's people may be thoroughly equipped for every good work" (2 Timothy 3:16-17, TNIV®). Christians generally view both the Old and New Testaments as God-breathed, or inspired by God, although there is a wide range of beliefs about the nature of God's inspiration and the identity of the persons who wrote the Bible. When I was young, I thought Moses wrote the first part of the Bible, David wrote the middle part, and that Jesus and Paul wrote the last part. I know now that those who wrote down the stories of Moses, David, and Jesus did so to inspire right relationship with God and one's neighbor. Paul's letters, concerned primarily with specific issues in the various churches, also inspire love of God, self, and neighbor. God inspired the words of the stories, histories, poetry, letters, and teachings in the Bible, and through them, continues to inspire our faith development.

> Read 2 Timothy 3:16-17 in two or three different translations (NIV, NRSV, KJV, etc.). What does it mean to you that the Bible was "inspired by God"?

The Old and New Testaments

The Hebrew Bible, referred to as the Old Testament by many Christians, emerged out of the life and faith of the Hebrew people, the Israelites. These people are the ancestors of modern Judaism, which is the faith of Jewish people today. The New Testament emerged out of the life and faith of the followers of Jesus, who were Jewish. In its beginnings, Christianity was a sect within Judaism, made up of people who believed Jesus was the long-awaited Jewish messiah, or christ. Both the Hebrew word *Messiah* and Greek word *Christ* mean "the Anointed One," which was originally a reference to the anointing of a new king.

> Read the Great Commandment in Matthew 22:34-40; Mark 12:28-34; and Luke 10:25-28. Then, read Deuteronomy 6:5 and Leviticus 19:18. How do these Scriptures illustrate the common threads and themes of the Bible? What do they say to you about Jesus and his grounding in the Hebrew Bible?

Thus, our Bible is the product of a faith "co-op," a cooperative venture between God, the Creator of the universe, and two faith communities of the Hebrew people and the early Christian church. Christians recognize the distinctive nature of these two collections of sacred writings as well as an inherent connectedness that provides some common threads and themes that are woven together throughout Scripture.

Many Years and Many Writers

The Bible is a collection, or library, of books. The writing of the Bible spans a period of 1500 to 2000 years and involved countless hands and hearts. Much of the Bible, however, did not begin in written form. Some of the Old Testament stories lived for centuries in oral form. Eventually, as these stories were recorded, the written and oral material flowed together. The stories and writings express how those who collected and wrote the stories understood and related to God.

> What stories have been important to your family or community? How have they influenced your understanding of yourself, your family, or your community? What, if anything, do they reflect about God?

There were countless, often unknown, contributors to the process of writing the Bible. There were, however, some obvious major figures. Genesis, Exodus, Leviticus, Numbers, and Deuteronomy are known as the *Pentateuch*, which means "five scrolls." These books have traditionally been attributed to Moses. When I was a young person, I had the image of a stenographer following Moses around, writing down everything he said and did or that Moses himself penned the first five books. Now, I find it more accurate to say these books were written about

> What do you think of the image of the co-op as a way of thinking about God's inspiration through many biblical writers over hundreds of years? What other images would you use? What connections do you see between faith development and the writing of the Bible by many people over hundreds of years?

Moses and in his honor. They are full of his stories, sayings, and quotes.[1] The same is true of the relationship between the Psalms and King David, who is remembered not only as a king, but as a singer and songwriter. Surely, some of David's work is captured in the Psalms.[2] I've come to believe that, in his honor, unknown writers produced some of what are commonly called the "Psalms of David." That's the way life works in a co-op. People work together, giving honor to their heroes, although much of the grunt work is done behind the scenes—anonymous, unnoticed, and without fanfare or credit. Everyone in the faith co-op we call the biblical community of faith would say, "To God be the glory!"

Jahweh, Elohim, Deuteronomists, and Priests

In the course of your biblical studies, you may have run across the letters JEDP. Each of these letters represents a major stream of biblical authorship, or more accurately, *editor*ship. In the Old Testament, several Hebrew words are used for the Deity. Many scholars think these various names for God represent different strands of the biblical tradition. For example, when a biblical passage uses the word "Elohim," or "El," for God, it most likely reflects one strand of the biblical tradition. Likewise, when a passage uses the word "Yahweh," or "Yah," for God, this may reflect another strand of the tradition. As "Yahweh" is sometimes spelled "Jahweh," the "J" tradition represents material containing the "Yahweh" name, whereas the "E" tradition represents the material using "Elohim."

I call my wife by the name she was given at birth, "Cathey." It's the name her parents use when they speak to or about her. Earlier in her life, she was given a nickname, Barkley, which is actually her maiden name. Many of her friends know her as "Barkley," and others know her as "Cathey." Depending on the name one uses for her, I can tell the point in or the context of Cathey's life when that particular friendship was formed. The JEDP theory follows a similar concept. The "J" and "E" traditions are quite ancient, and they have been woven together and incorporated into the biblical stories by later editors. Now, our question of who wrote the Bible must stretch to also consider who *edited* the Bible. Let's look at two groups of editors of the Old Testament, represented by the last two letters of the JEDP formula.

The "D" tradition includes Deuteronomy, Joshua, Judges, First and Second Samuel, and First and Second Kings. Many scholars refer to the writers or editors of this material as the "Deuteronomistic historians." They wrote during the reign of King Josiah (640–609 B.C.). It was a time of religious reform during which many shrines to foreign gods were dismantled. The Temple in Jerusalem gained renewed prominence. This revival was launched when a scroll was discovered in the Temple in 621 B.C. Many scholars agree that this scroll was the Book of Deuteronomy. The Old Testament as we know it began to take its final shape during Josiah's reign.[3]

The prophet Jeremiah was either one of the Deuteronomistic historians or he began his work during the height of their influence. If among them, Jeremiah may have had a hand in editing some of the material from the "D" tradition. The Book of Jeremiah reveals the scope of his influence. The prophet lived a long life and wrote during both good times and bad—his work covering the time of religious reform and political expansion of Josiah's reign as well as the fall of Jerusalem and the Babylonian Exile. Jeremiah was a major voice in the Hebrew Bible.[4]

The "P" material was written during and after the Babylonian Exile (587–538 B.C.), which occurred just following the reign of King Josiah. The process of writing down the sacred stories continued and was made more urgent by the Exile to Babylon. The displaced Israelites feared that their children would intermarry with Babylonians and that they might never see Jerusalem again. Scholars refer to those who shaped the Scriptures during this period as the "Priestly" writers.[5] Sometimes they edited ancient stories. Sometimes they created new ones. Psalm 137 comes out of this period and reflects the agony of the Exile and the Israelites' depth of feeling against their Babylonian captors.[6]

The New Testament

When we explore the question of who wrote the Bible, Paul looms large as a major contributor to the New Testament. He is significant for many reasons, including his articulate description of God's grace, which he experienced through Jesus. He made an enormous evangelistic impact by spreading the gospel in Asia Minor, Greece, and Rome. Paul stands as the great interpreter of the meaning of Jesus in light of the Hebrew tradition.

The letters of Paul are the earliest material in the New Testament. Though the Gospels describe events that happened before Paul wrote, they were not put into the form we know until after Paul's letters were written.[7] Paul's words about Jesus focus on Christ's death, resurrection, and the encounter Paul had with the risen Christ on the road to Damascus.

As with the Old Testament, there are many unknown contributors to the New Testament. For example, the letter to the Hebrews was written anonymously; and some think John, the Gospel-writer, wrote Revelation, while others think another John wrote it.

Think for a moment about how these New Testament writers, particularly Paul, have shaped our history and even our vocabulary. An enduring metaphor for the church is "the body of Christ," as expressed by Paul in

1 Corinthians 12:27. A Christian today might begin or end a correspondence with the words of Romans 1:7, "Grace to you and peace!" Martin Luther launched the Protestant Reformation in part due to the influence of Paul's affirmation that our relationship with God is based on grace through Christ rather than the performance of good deeds, for which the traditional term is "justification by grace" through

> What other evidence do you see of the effects of New Testament language on our history and culture?

faith, as found in Romans 3:24. Even many Protestant churches are named "Grace." Churches in the Wesleyan tradition may include the name "Aldersgate," in honor of John Wesley's memorable experience with grace on May 24, 1738, at a Moravian meetinghouse on Aldersgate Street in London. Wesley writes about hearing someone read Luther's *Preface to the Epistle of St. Paul to the Romans*: "About a quarter before nine, while he was describing the change which God works in the heart through faith in Christ, I felt my heart strangely warmed. I felt I did trust in Christ, Christ alone, for salvation; and an assurance was given me that He had taken away *my* sins, even *mine*, and saved *me* from the law of sin and death."[8]

The Gospels

Each of the Gospels in the New Testament was anonymously written. Nothing in the texts indicates the writers' names. However, there are authorship traditions associated with each of the Gospels that date back to the earliest days of the church.

Some scholars think Mark is rooted in stories about Jesus told by John Mark, one of the early followers we read about in the book of Acts. Another of the early traditions concerning this Gospel maintains that it was influenced by Peter. Some see it as the stories of Peter in the words of John Mark. Regardless, the anonymous writer, known to the reader as "Mark," made an important contribution by writing what was most likely the earliest Gospel, setting the tone for what was to follow. Mark seemed to write from a tightly woven and finely crafted outline, which was followed by Matthew and Luke. The earliest known Gospel manuscripts were written in Greek and are themselves copies of even earlier manuscripts that were either destroyed or buried somewhere under Middle Eastern sand.[9] So with this brief introduction, we begin to see the communal nature of biblical authorship. But it runs even deeper than this.

Mark reveals that during the short period of time between the events of Jesus' life and the writing of the Gospels, the Jesus stories were translated from Aramaic to Greek. Mark 5:41 says, "He took her by the hand and said to her, '*Talitha cum*,' which means 'Little girl, get up!'" The usage of Aramaic in this Scripture gives us a clue about how the story was passed on to us. The native language of Jesus, Peter, and John Mark would have been Aramaic, a form of Hebrew commonly spoken over much of that part of the world. Within Aramaic, there were many variations and local phrases. We still see this today, despite the homogenizing impact of cable television. Various pockets of the United States have colloquial expressions unique to those regions. In his book *Rabbi Jesus*, Bruce Chilton explains the nature of *targums*, or teachings about Torah. He writes that every little community had their own unique targums, or expressions of the oral law. As a carpenter, Jesus would have traveled through the region and picked up many of these local targums from various places.[10]

Jesus and the disciples may have been able to speak or read some Greek. Some Jewish synagogues used the Hebrew version of the Bible (our Old Testament) and others used a Greek translation of the Bible. If the Scriptures in their synagogues were in Hebrew, their Greek would have been limited to dealings in the marketplace (that is, the building trade for Jesus, the fishing business for Peter, Andrew, James, and John). If the Scriptures in their synagogues were in Greek, then Jesus and his disciples may have been more familiar with that language.[11]

> Look up the following verses in Mark: 5:41 (*Talitha cum*); 7:11 (*Corban*); 7:34 (*ephphatha*); 14:36 (*abba*); 15:22 (*Golgatha*); and 15:34 (*Eloi, Eloi, lema sabachthani*). In each case, the Gospel writer gives the Greek translation of the meaning of these Aramaic expressions. Why do you think these Aramaic words were preserved in the story? Which of these Aramaic expressions has the most meaning for your faith? Why?

So, how did the New Testament stories get from Aramaic to Greek? You see a hint of this in the Scripture cited above. The writer departs from the Greek to quote Jesus in the original language, Aramaic: "He took her by the hand and said to her, '*Talitha cum*,' which means 'Little girl, get up!'" The two words "which means" let us know that the writer of Mark, operating in the Greek language, gives us a brief quote from Jesus' original Aramaic, which he translates into Greek because many in his audience (perhaps an early Christian congregation in Rome) would not have been familiar with Aramaic. We can conclude, then, that there is a step of translation from Aramaic to Greek that occurred before the Gospel of Mark was written.

Matthew 28:11-15 includes a little detail that I didn't notice for many years. According to Matthew, these verses tell of an early Christian rebuttal to a plan devised by the priests and elders to account for the stone being rolled away from Jesus' tomb. Matthew writes that the religious leaders of Jerusalem bribed the Roman soldiers in charge of guarding the tomb to say, "'[Jesus'] disciples came by night and stole him away while we were asleep.'" It is at the close of the story that Matthew imparts to us a small detail when he writes that "this story is still told among the Jews *to this day*," indicating that a considerable amount of time had passed between the event being described (the resurrection of Christ) and the actual writing of Matthew's Gospel (28:15, italics added).

> Read Matthew 27:62-66 and 28:11-15. Why do you think the Gospel writer includes this story about extra security around Jesus' tomb and the subsequent plot? What do these verses say to you about the concerns of the writer?

Luke understood the global implications of Jesus' actions, and he writes with a power and style that leave me spellbound at times. The opening words of both Luke and Acts make it clear that the books were written by the same person and that Acts was intended to be a sequel to Luke. The vocabulary and style of writing of the two documents also match. Luke's sequel, Acts, carries the story beyond Jesus into the early years of the church—notably featuring Paul as a leading character in this drama.

A significant yet subtle shift occurs in Acts 16 that gives us some insight into the writer of Luke and Acts.[12] For the first fifteen chapters of Acts, the writer uses the third-person (*he, she,* or *they*) to describe the action. Then with 16:10, the writer shifts to the first-person, using *us* and *we*. There are four such "we" passages in Acts.[13] From the early days of the church, many Christians have believed that the writer of the Books of Luke and Acts was a traveling companion and coworker of Paul, as Luke is mentioned in Colossians 4:14. If this ancient tradition of authorship is accurate, and I see no reason to doubt it, then it means Paul's influence in the writing of the New Testament includes not only the letters attributed to him but also the major two-volume work we know as Luke and Acts.

There were many early Christian traditions and legends about the various disciples of Jesus. One tradition holds that the Gospel of John was written by John, son of Zebedee. He and his brother James, along with another set of fishermen brothers, Andrew and Simon, were the first disciples called by Jesus. Scholars place the writing of the Gospel of John sometime around A.D. 80–90, which

Imagine that you are a traveling companion of Paul and the writer of Acts. Read Acts 21:1-18. What would you have thought when Paul decided to go to Jerusalem in spite of the danger there? How would it have felt to be welcomed warmly by the leaders of the church in Jerusalem or to meet James, the brother of Jesus and leader of the Christians in Jerusalem? Who might have been among the elders present in Acts 21:18?

would be roughly around the time that Matthew and Luke were written or perhaps a few years later.[14]

Two things have always puzzled me about the Gospel of John. Why does John talk about "the Jews" as if they were a separate group of people, when in most cases everyone in the story is Jewish? And why does Jesus seem different in this Gospel compared to how he is described in Matthew, Mark, and Luke? I began to make sense of these two issues by thinking what it would have been like for the disciple John to write this Gospel during the first century. How might an old man remember stories from his youth? The other Gospels record conflicts between Jesus and some of the religious leaders (that is, the Pharisees), but in John's Gospel, the struggle is with "the Jews." The stories in the Gospel of John take place during a time of painful conflict and division between traditional Judaism and what was emerging as Christianity. John's Gospel reflects this "us versus them" worldview. His term, "the Jews," was technically inaccurate because Jesus and almost everyone in the stories were thoroughly Jewish and were part of the Jewish community. However, when John's Gospel was actually written, the distinction was real, making it apparent that John's perception of "the Jews" reflected the status of the situation as he saw it.[15]

Now to tackle the second question. If the disciple John is the writer, we have an account from one of three men in Jesus' inner circle. Jesus may have said things to these three that he would not have said to the crowds. This helps me understand what Jesus says in John 14:6, which reads, "I am the way, and the truth, and the life. No one comes to the Father except through

Read John 14:1-6. Why do you think the writer of John would record this "I am" saying? How does it speak to you? How would you describe the way of Jesus? What, for you, is the most important truth that Jesus embodied? How do you understand the nature of the *life* found in Jesus?

me." I think these words were spoken originally to the twelve disciples or to the inner circle of Peter, James, and John. This scene in the Gospel of John is near Jesus' long speech, known as the "Farewell Discourse," which he also addresses to his inner circle of followers. In this speech, Jesus reassures and prepares his followers for his impending departure.

Returning to the Question

Here's a final reflection on the question "Who wrote the Bible?" It's a good and worthwhile question. Understanding who wrote a particular part of the Bible gives us valuable interpretive and contextual insights. The question quickly becomes "Who were the writers and the editors of the various parts of the Bible?" We join in an exciting, fascinating, and illuminating journey along with historians, archaeologists, linguists, and theologians.

If we directed the original question to God, asking in a spirit of prayer, what might be the answer? I don't think God would simply give us the answer to a technical question that has puzzled scholars, one such as whether the Book of Revelation was written by the author of the Gospel of John or someone else named John. I think the answer would be something like that received by Moses at Mount Sinai.

If we were to ask, as Moses did, "If they ask me who wrote this book, what shall I say to them?" I think the answer would be something like this: "The Bible speaks for itself." Or, "The Bible stands on its own merits." Or, "The Bible is what it is." Or, "Tell them I wrote it for them—'for teaching, for reproof, for correction, and for training in righteousness, so that everyone ... may be proficient, equipped for every good work'" (2 Timothy 3:16). This brings us back to the answer children would give in Sunday school if asked, "Who wrote the Bible?" They would say, "God."

Maybe God's answer to our question would be, "I did." What if we pressed the matter and said, "And who are you?" We might hear something like what Moses heard in Exodus 3:14, when God said to him, "I AM WHO I AM.... Thus you shall say to the Israelites, 'I AM has sent me to you.'"

Closing

Imagine we are around a campfire on a clear night, hearing your grandfather tell us a story that his grandfather had told him. It's a story about Abraham and Sarah. It goes back more generations than anyone can count, and those of us sitting around the campfire have heard it enough times that we've memorized the story. But the story hasn't yet been written. In fact, no one around the campfire can read. Some day it will be written, but for now, we are a people of trained ears, clear memories, and uncluttered minds. We have hundreds of stories like this one. We know them all. They tell the story of who we are and whose we are. Someday, in the far distant future, someone will ask a question that, to us, seems quite strange: "Who wrote the Bible?" We are not yet a book-people nor are we a writing-people. We are a *story-people*. We believe these stories are gifts from God. They are in our hearts. We hold them sacred and treasure them. They are *our* stories. In them we find our identity and meaning for our lives. As a closing prayer, read Deuteronomy 26:5b-10a.

Notes

[1] See more about the formation of the first five books of the Bible in "Introduction to the Pentateuch," by Joseph Blenkinsopp, in *The New Interpreter's Bible*, Vol. I (Abingdon Press, 2001); pages 308–09.

[2] See "The Book of Psalms," by J. Clinton McCann, Jr., in *The New Interpreter's Bible*, Vol. IV; page 643.

[3] See 2 Kings 22–23:27. See also *The New Oxford Annotated Bible*, third edition, edited by Michael D. Coogan (Oxford University Press, 2001); page 310 HB.

[4] For more about Jeremiah and the historical context of Josiah's reform, see "The Book of Jeremiah," by Patrick D. Miller, Jr., in *The New Interpreter's Bible*, Vol. VI; pages 555–63.

[5] For further reading on the JEDP theory, see "Modern Source Theories," in *The New Oxford Annotated Bible*; pages 4–6 HB. For more on the Documentary Hypothesis concerning JEDP, see *Harper's Bible Dictionary*, edited by Paul J. Achtemeier (HarperSanFrancisco, 1985); pages 985–86.

[6] For more about how the Deuteronomistic and Priestly traditions continued side-by-side during the Exile, see *Theology of the Old Testament: Testimony, Dispute, Advocacy*, by Walter Brueggemann (Fortress Press, 1997); pages 670–74.

[7] For a chronology of Paul's letter and how they interface with Acts, see "Introduction to Epistolary Literature," by Robert W. Wall, in *The New Interpreter's Bible*, Vol. X; pages 372–74.

[8] From *John Wesley's Theology Today: A Study of the Wesleyan Tradition in Light of Current Theological Dialogue,* by Colin W. Williams (Abingdon, 1960); page 105. And for more on the writings of Luther, see *Martin Luther's Preface to the Epistle of St. Paul to the Romans,* by Martin Luther (Discipleship Resources, 1977).

[9] See *The New Interpreter's Study Bible* (Abingdon Press, 2003); pages 1801–03.

[10] *Rabbi Jesus: An Intimate Biography,* by Bruce Chilton (Doubleday, 2000); pages xviii, 4–5, and 20.

[11] See "The Gospel of Luke," by R. Alan Culpepper, in *The New Interpreter's Bible,* Vol. IX; page 105.

[12] See *The New Interpreter's Study Bible*; pages 1953–54.

[13] Acts 16:10-17; 20:5-15; 21:1-18; 27:1–28:16.

[14] See *The New Oxford Annotated Bible*; pages 146–47 NT. For a more extensive discussion about the authorship of the Gospel of John, see "The Gospel of John," by Gail R. O'Day, in *The New Interpreter's Bible,* Vol. IX; pages 498–500. And for more about the Johannine traditions, see "John the Apostle," *The HarperCollins Bible Dictionary,* edited by Paul J. Achtemeier (HarperSanFrancisco, 1985); pages 537–38; *The Master's Men,* by William Barclay (Abingdon Press, 1959); pages 29–40; and *The Oxford Dictionary of Saints,* by David Hugh Farmer, third edition (Oxford University Press, 1992); pages 256–57.

[15] See *The New Interpreter's Study Bible*; page 1906. Leander Keck explains the tension between Jesus and the Pharisees in his video presentation, "Session Nineteen: Mounting Controversy," in DISCIPLE: BECOMING DISCIPLES THROUGH BIBLE STUDY, second edition (Abingdon Press, 1993).

CHAPTER 2
HOW IS THE BIBLE AUTHORITATIVE FOR MEMBERS OF THE FAITH COMMUNITY?

Focus: This chapter explores some of the ways people of faith read the Bible and find within it guidance and meaning for their daily lives. It will help us affirm our ways of reading and interpreting the Bible as we respect the various and perhaps quite different ways other people read and interpret it.

Gathering

Greet one another. Write the word "Authority" on a large sheet of newsprint or white paper. Tape this to a wall or other easily accessible location. Ask the question, "Can you name a time when you had a change of attitude or a change in your behavior because of the Bible?" Write responses to the question on the newsprint. Review the written responses with others in the group. As an opening prayer, sing or read "Thy Word Is a Lamp Unto My Feet."

Pray the following prayer together: Loving God, guide us as we explore ways that reading and interpreting the Bible can nourish our faith. Give us respect for one another even as we differ in our ways of reading and understanding. In Christ we pray. Amen.

In our last session, we explored the question "Who wrote the Bible?" Our approach was analytical. This session will be more anecdotal and reflective. You are invited to ask the question "How is the Bible authoritative for me?"

John Wesley was the founder of the Methodist movement out of which several denominations eventually emerged. Wesley examined faith questions in light of four considerations: Scripture, tradition, reason, and experience.[1] In our first session about who wrote the Bible, we looked for clues within Scripture itself. We also consulted other voices in the history of Christian tradition. This session will focus more on reason—how people process biblical material to formulate beliefs and doctrines. This session also will focus on our experience—how the Bible is authoritative for us in our daily lives.

This session will also be relational as we consider how other people experience the Bible as authoritative for their lives.

The Bible's Authority and Our Experience

Our experience shapes the authority of the Bible. My first Bible was an edition of the King James Version that included color photographs of Michelangelo's paintings and sculptures. Those photographs, especially those of Michelangelo's *Pieta*, the sculpture of Jesus' mother holding Christ's dead body, and Michelangelo's sculpture of Moses, with its long, flowing beard and piercing eyes, enhanced my emotional connection to the Scriptures. As a young child, I developed an awareness of God's presence and a sense of being in a relationship with God, who was for me a loving, caring presence in my life and in the world.

What are your early memories of the Bible?

I have studied the Bible with hundreds of people through the years, and I have noticed that those who develop an early, loving relationship with God tend to learn bits and pieces of the Bible that focus on establishing and maintaining a relationship of trust and prayer. How far one goes with this depends on countless variables. Some people become very familiar with the Bible. Some may not get much beyond the Lord's Prayer,

What is your favorite version of Psalm 23? Do you know one of these versions by heart? What other Scriptures do you know by heart?

"Golden Rule," or the Twenty-third Psalm. Most people who have attended church worship services or small group ministries absorb more biblical knowledge than they realize, even though they may not be confident in their understanding of the Scriptures.

Some people's early religious experiences are dominated by themes of divine judgment. I have known people with this background who turned away from the Bible in their youth and then began as adults to reluctantly re-engage the Bible in study. For these people, the Bible's authority was experienced primarily in negative, "thou shalt not" ways. Sometimes the process of letting go of these images is painful, and sometimes it is liberating.

> THE GOLDEN RULE
> "In everything do to others as you would have them do to you; for this is the law and the prophets." This saying of Jesus, found in Matthew 7:12, is often called the "Golden Rule." It calls for activity on behalf of others. A variation is attributed to Rabbi Hillel, who lived during the first century B.C. and said, "What is hateful to you do not do to your neighbor; that is the whole Torah . . . go and learn it."[2]

Because the image of God as parent is basic to biblical faith, a person who has had parental trauma in early life may resist giving the Bible authority in his or her life. Many years ago, a college student came to my office for counsel. I suggested she formulate and pray a personal "breath prayer." A breath prayer is a short petition, such as "God, keep me simple." She sought *peace*, so "give me peace" was her petition. I asked, "What name do you typically use for the Deity in prayer: God, Lord, Father?" She said, assertively, "Not 'Father'!" I said, "Okay, what would you prefer?" She replied, "Coach." Her prayer was, "Coach, give me peace." I suggested she pray that prayer as often as possible for a week and then we would talk about her experience. A week later I asked how the prayer went. She said, "After two days, I realized it was silly to call God, 'Coach.'" Her prayer changed to, "Father, give me peace." Then she told me that her father had been killed in an accident early in her life. As a child, she blamed God for her dad's death and she had not been able to call God "Father." For the first time in many years, she could pray to God as "Father."

The Bible contains other images for God in addition to that of "Father," which may be helpful to those who have difficulty with the idea of God as Father. Some of these images are rock (1 Samuel 2:2; Psalm 95:1), mother (Isaiah 66:13), eagle (Deuteronomy 32:11-12), fortress (Psalm 31:3), potter (Isaiah 64:8b), water (Jeremiah 2:13;

> What biblical images of God are most helpful to you? How are they helpful? What do they reveal to you about God?

17:13; John 4:10-15), and light (Isaiah 60:19-20; 1 John 1:5). No single biblical image or metaphor says all that can be known about God, yet each reveals truth and communicates something of value about the nature of God. Such biblical images for God may help those who might otherwise struggle with the authority of the Bible in their lives.

The Bible's Authority and Our Reason

Our God-given capacity for reason also shapes the authority of the Bible. In Bible studies, I have encountered people who had very little religious training as children and enter adulthood with almost no knowledge of the Bible. These people often make the best students. They may not have a strong emotional attachment to biblical authority. Some of them approach the Bible more from the standpoint of *reason*, the way they might approach a course in Western Civilization. As they study the Bible, and as their relationship with God deepens, the Bible assumes authority in their lives, and it begins to impact their attitudes, their behavior, and their decision-making.

Another way of understanding how reason operates in our faith is simply to notice the different ways people think about the Bible. The way a person thinks regarding the Bible provides a clue about how the Bible is authoritative for that person. It is always fun to have an engineer in a Bible study. I once was the pastor of a church full of engineers. They were excellent Bible students, and some of them were able to express a need that seemed to be rather common among engineers—the Bible spoke to the non-analytical side of their brain that needed some exercise (that is, the arena of emotions and intuition). Some, but not all, of them had difficulty reading the Bible poetically or symbolically, rather than literally.

If one's primary mode of thinking is historical, one will find the Bible's authority in historical events, such as the deliverance from exile in Babylon or the crucifixion of Jesus. If one tends to think literally, then the Bible's authority may be expressed in such phrases as, "The Bible says it. I believe it. That settles it." Christians have a history of grouping themselves with like-minded believers. Persons with a literal understanding of the Bible and those who read the Bible more poetically or symbolically may lose patience with each other! Different understandings of biblical authority in a class or congregation can, however, can be mutually enriching, that is, if everyone is gentle and respectful.

Thinking Biblically

The Bible is authoritative for people in the faith community in ways that are not always obvious. If a person reads the Bible with some degree of frequency, participates in worship where the Scriptures are read and Scripture-based hymns are sung, and engages in occasional or regular small group learning experiences in church, that person will begin to think biblically.

Honesty requires the acknowledgement that the Bible is a large document with many different strands of tradition representing various understandings of God and a wide range of human experi-

> Try this simple spiritual exercise to consider how the Bible is authoritative for you: List the ten biblical passages that are most important to you. If you are a Bible-underliner, notice those passages that you keep revisiting. Why are those particular passages helpful to you? What is the understanding of God reflected in those passages? How do those passages shape your self-understanding and your outlook toward the world and the future?

ence. Depending on one's perspective, experiences, and the kind of faith community one joins, one can "think biblically" in many different ways. There are plenty of biblical passages that reflect strong themes of judgment, a negative view of the world, a circle-the-wagons worldview to protect the people of God from those outside the fellowship, and a foreboding outlook toward the future. Conversely, one can "think biblically" by finding the many biblical passages that reflect themes of forgiveness and grace; an understanding of God's love that embraces all creation; an inviting, inclusive attitude toward everyone; and an attitude toward the future that is confident, full of hope, and sees those in the faith community as "more than conquerors" (Romans 8:37).

Both of these contrasting approaches to life can find justification in Scripture, as can many other attitudes and perspectives. The nature of the Bible's authority for a person depends on several factors, including how one interprets the Bible and the biblical passages, stories, and themes that one emphasizes.

The Nature of the Bible's Authority

Some Christians, who see the Bible as a rulebook, develop precise attitudes to be taken and behaviors to be performed in order to live according to the Bible. Some Christians see the Bible as a guidebook and order their lives around certain principles, such as the Great Commandment of Luke 10:27 that says, "You shall love the Lord your God with all your heart, and with all your soul, and with all your strength, and with all your mind; and your neighbor as yourself." And some Christians see the Bible as a storybook, finding inspiration and hope in the powerful stories of the Bible.

Many Protestant branches of the Christian family use the historic approach of affirming the sufficiency of the Bible for matters of life and faith. In 1870, a Roman Catholic "Vatican Council declared that the pope is infallible when speaking ex cathedra on questions of faith and morals."[3] It was after this declaration that Protestants countered with the claim that the Bible is infallible. This has led to all kinds of debates and doctrines about the nature of the Bible itself.

Some people have been taught at an early age that the historical narratives of the Hebrew Bible should be read as literal history and that any other interpretation would somehow undermine the validity of the entire Bible. When it comes to biblical authority, sometimes a person's most basic concern is that the Bible be treated with reverence and respect, that it be understood as God's inspired Word, and that it be viewed as offering salvation. Some have bought into terms such as inerrancy or infallibility because they have heard people use these words to describe the Bible's importance.

> How is the Bible is authoritative for you in the various areas of your life, both as an individual and as part of a community of faith?

However, after one realizes that there are many approaches to the Bible that treat the texts with reverence and respect, that hear the Scripture as God's inspired Word, and that find salvation within the pages of the Bible, it may be possible to rethink the implications of using such terms as inerrant or infallible with regard to these sacred texts. For some people, it is liberating to know one can revere the Bible without suspending one's common sense or inquiring mind.[4]

Let us consider four broad areas of life: relationships, ethics, economics, and politics. Relationally, how is the Bible authoritative for you in your dealings with others? Do you shun or avoid those who disagree with you? Are you committed to work for reconciliation with all people? Are your attitudes toward others rooted in grace and forgiveness? Do you embrace what Brian McLaren calls "a generous orthodoxy"?[5]

Ethically, how does the Bible inform your understanding of right and wrong? Does the Bible inspire you to be a more honest human being? How does the Bible influence your daily actions and behavior? Is your commitment of justice enhanced by the Bible? Does your biblical faith make you more aware of injustice?

Economically, are you committed to tithing as an expression of your gratitude? Are you committed to frugality as an expression of simple living? Are you committed to ecological conservation as an expression of stewardship?

Politically, has the Bible shaped your understanding of citizenship— both as a citizen of the world and as a citizen of your country? How has the Bible shaped your political attitudes? Do you believe American principles of democracy are consistent with the Bible and seem to flow out of the Bible? How has the Bible challenged you to look beyond your own interests and to try to understand what is in the best interest of all?

> Psalm 119:105:
>
> "Your word is a lamp to my feet and a light to my path."
>
> "By your words I can see where I'm going; they throw a beam of light on my dark path" (*Message*).

These are just some of the areas of life where the Bible "comforts the afflicted and afflicts the comfortable." As one of the comfortable, the Bible consistently challenges my presuppositions and prejudices. The Bible offers a window into a more global worldview and calls us away from our comfort zones. While this may make us squirm, the Bible also provides light for our path.

Biblical Authority in Today's World

Our busy lives are inundated with competing ideologies from today's electronic media—news, commentary, and marketing. They seek our time, our resources, and our energy. They seek to shape our attitudes and preferences. Which is more authoritative for us: the Bible, talk radio, or television shows like *Desperate Housewives* or *Survivor*?

Does your worldview shape your understanding of the Bible and the Christian faith? Or, do the Bible and your Christian faith shape your worldview? Today's world raises these questions regarding biblical authority.

Occasionally, someone in a Bible study group will question whether serious biblical study is wise: "I'm afraid that if I seriously study the Bible, it will cause more doubt than faith." This is a real, honest, and valid concern for some because serious Bible study may shake the foundations upon which one's childhood faith is built.

Biblical Scholarship and Biblical Truth

For example, most of us have been taught that the Bible is trustworthy and that we can depend on what the Bible says to be true. We read 1 Timothy 1:1, which begins, "Paul, an apostle of Christ Jesus ..." Then we read a commentary such as the one found in the *Access Bible*, which states, "First Timothy asserts that it was written by Paul (1:1), but as noted [elsewhere] ... this is almost certainly not the case."[6]

This kind of commentary throws some people for a loop, perhaps causing one to think that if such scholarship can be avoided, one's faith will be more secure. When a person comes to this point, it is helpful to ask, "What *are* the foundations of my faith?" Questions, like "Who wrote First or Second Timothy?" are helpful for understanding the context, the original intent of the author, and the interpretation of the letter by the original recipient(s); but the truth inherent in the text and the text's ultimate value for the reader do not depend on who wrote it. Scholarly assessments of "who wrote what" shift through the ages as archaeologists find more data under the sand and as linguists learn more about the ancient Hebrew, Aramaic, and Greek languages. We need not fear scholarship or historical research. It is helpful to remember that the work of biblical scholars is vital, but it is not the last word. They provide tools, not the foundation for our faith, which is rooted in a relationship of grace offered by God through Christ. Don't confuse the hammer and saw with the piece of wood you're working with!

Some people have an apocalyptic view of biblical authority. "Apocalyptic" is a style of writing—a genre of literature found in the Bible and elsewhere. The title of the last book of the Bible, in its original Greek language, is *Apocalypse*, which is translated as "Revelation" in English. Apocalyptic literature reflects a worldview that sees little or no hope in the structures of society. Hope, rather, comes through direct, divine intervention into history. An apocalyptic mind sees everything in terms of good vs. evil.

One of the characteristics of apocalyptic literature is a focus on things eschatological. *Eschaton* is the Greek word for "last things." The popular *Left Behind* books are fiction, based upon apocalyptic and eschatological worldviews. That is, they portray a particular "revelation" of the end of time.

We may be entering into an era when apocalyptic thinking will become more and more prominent in society. The popularity of the *Left Behind* books is due in large part to our society's increasing doubt in the ability of social structures to function in an acceptable manner. Apocalyptic thinking gives a religious interpretation to our sometimes-chaotic world and to natural disasters, such as hurricanes and earthquakes, and to human disasters, like war and terrorism.

Today's world is rediscovering an ancient truth that grace is meaningless without a concept of judgment and a healthy appreciation for sin. The proclamation of grace, forgiveness, and self-giving love requires an awareness of, and appreciation for, the human experience of what the *Star Wars* movies call "the dark side of the force." The Gospel must connect with,

> How can a largely non-apocalyptic congregation relate to people within the congregation or within the community who tend to see the world in apocalyptic terms?

engage, and provide an alternative to and a way out of the human experiences of hopelessness, estrangement, evil, and sin.

Churches and Biblical Authority

We are often unaware of ways the Bible is authoritative for us. Some of the patterns of the faith community are biblical, yet we may go about our lives unaware that the way we operate is rooted in Scripture. Church architecture has been influenced by synagogue architecture, which was influenced by the Jerusalem Temple, which was influenced by the portable Tabernacle of the Old Testament. Many churches have a narthex, which in the early days of the church was where those preparing for membership would worship. I once visited a monastery chapel that was designed with a small nave, or sanctuary, and a very large narthex, as there were often more visitors in worship than monks. Much of today's Christian worship has roots in biblical practices, such as praying, singing, presenting offerings at the altar, hearing Scriptures, and listening to Scripture-based commentaries or sermons.

Church organization varies among the denominations, but today's bishops, elders, and deacons have their origins in the letters of the New Testament. Church budgets are driven both on the income-side, by such biblical concepts as first fruits and tithe (Deuteronomy 26), and on the expense-side, by the New Testament practice of giving offerings and caring for widows (Acts 2:44-45; 1 Timothy 5:3-17).

Church vocabulary has been shaped by the Bible. One of the challenges facing the church today is to translate church vocabulary into language that non-Christians can understand. The word *tithe* isn't part of the marketplace today. Last year, we asked our sixth grade confirmation class to define the word *grace*, and we received a wide range of answers.

> What additional evidences of biblical authority can you identify in your church?

Some of them nailed it, and some of them reflected the same general use of this term that we see in the secular world, as in the "grace period" for credit cards.

Some of the ways we use a phrase like "the blood of Christ" must seem quite strange to non-Christians. Parts of Christian vocabulary are rooted in Jewish sacrificial practices that ended in the year A.D. 70 when the Romans destroyed the Temple, yet we still sing songs like, "There Is Power in the Blood." The earliest Christians (with their Jewish backgrounds) had no trouble with the idea that God had sent his Son to die for us, but many modern people would flee from a deity described that way. Fasting was a common biblical practice that is being rediscovered in today's world, though perhaps for health and weight loss reasons more often than as a discipline to enhance one's prayer focus.

The church's calendar, or "Christian year," with colors representing seasons like Lent and Advent, has biblical roots in the Hebrew calendar. As a store was closing one fall afternoon, I noticed an employee putting a sign on the door that said, "Closed—Religious Holiday." I realized the following day would be Yom Kippur, the "Day of Atonement," a holy day for Jews. I first learned about Yom Kippur through baseball. I remember when Sandy Koufax gave up his place in the starting rotation during a World Series because he wouldn't pitch on Yom Kippur.

Concluding Thoughts

As you can see, the Bible's authority expresses itself in a variety of ways. For all Christians, the authority of the Bible undergirds questions about life and faith. As we engage our reason, our experience, and what we have been taught about the Bible, we learn that "thinking biblically" reveals the One who offers life, mercy, hope, compassion, and salvation.

Closing

What are some of the foundational biblical texts that shape your understanding of God, inform your understanding of the role of the faith community, and give you an orientation for how to live your life? For some, it may be John 3:16. For others, it may be the "Sermon on the Mount" in Matthew 5–7 or the "love chapter" 1 Corinthians 13.

Read aloud Genesis 12:2b-3:
"I will bless you, and make your name great, so that you will be a blessing. . . . and in you all the families of the earth shall be blessed." Think prayerfully about how God's blessings, as revealed in biblical stories, can be authoritative for you in your life.

Close the session by singing again "Thy Word Is a Lamp Unto My Feet" or another song about God's Word.

Notes

[1] For more about this approach, see *John Wesley's Theology Today: A Study of the Wesleyan Tradition in Light of Current Theological Dialogue*, by Colin W. Williams (Abingdon, 1960); pages 23–38.

[2] See the footnote on Matthew 7:12 in *The New Oxford Annotated Bible*, third edition, edited by Michael D. Coogan (Oxford University Press, 2001); page 17 NT.

[3] See *A History of the Christian Church*, by Lars P. Qualben (Thomas Nelson and Sons, 1958); pages 379.

[4] For more, see *Taking the Bible Seriously*, by Leander Keck (Association Press, 1962). Keck helps the reader to struggle, wrestle, or argue with a biblical text as an act of respect for the text and for the One who inspired its writing.

[5] *A Generous Orthodoxy*, by Brian D. McLaren (Zondervan, 2004); page 31.

[6] From the introductory material of First Timothy in *The Access Bible*, edited by Gail R. O'Day and David Peterson (Oxford University Press, 1999); page 319.

CHAPTER 3
WHAT DOES THE BIBLE SAY
TO US ABOUT GOD, JESUS,
AND THE HOLY SPIRIT?

Focus: This session explores the Bible as the primary source for the Christian understanding of God.

Gathering

As an opening prayer, sing or read the hymn "O God in Heaven," "Come Thou Almighty King," or another favorite hymn about the Trinity. How does the hymn help you understand the Christian concept of God as Trinity?

Pray the following prayer together: God, help us as we explore your triune nature as God, Jesus, and Holy Spirit in the Bible. Renew us. Help us to know more fully who you are. In Christ we pray. Amen.

What Does the Bible Say About God?

The biblical story encompasses a broad geographical area. Biblical people interacted with, and were influenced by, a variety of cultures and religions. This occurred over a lengthy period of history, from the time of Abraham and Sarah (roughly 2000 B.C. to 1700 B.C.) to the years following the destruction of Jerusalem by the Romans in A.D. 70.[1] The Bible is a lengthy and complex document that reflects considerable diversity of beliefs about and experiences of God. Any summary of what the Bible says about God is an act of biblical interpretation.

In the video presentation, "The Biblical Word," Dr. Albert Outler offers an interpretive summary of what the Bible says about God, finding that "there is a single primal narrative that runs through the whole Bible ... a coherent, consistent message ... about the sovereign grace of the one God and the radical contrast between the power syndrome and the rule of grace."[2] As I interpret these biblical teachings about the sovereign grace of God, I may proclaim that God's grace is the cornerstone of my faith, but if those I care about experience me as judgmental or focused on God's wrath, then there's a definite disconnect between my stated biblical interpretation and my operative biblical understanding. I believe everyone, either consciously or unconsciously, gives greater weight to particular parts of the Bible. We tend to interpret some parts of the Bible in light of other parts.

> Write down your five most important beliefs. Find a partner and compare your lists. What is the source of your beliefs? Where did you learn what you believe? What role does the Bible play in your beliefs? What biblical passages about God are most important to you?

When I step back and look at the broad sweep of Scripture, a few truths come to mind: God is sovereign over the universe. God is involved, or engaged, with humanity. God has created us and partnered, or covenanted, with us.[3] And God guides us and cares for us, individually and collectively, as illustrated by the common biblical image of shepherd. Based on these teachings, the Bible extends to human life, expectations of conduct, and ethics (i.e., setting boundaries via "statutes" and "ordinances," as in Deuteronomy 4:5-8), all with an eye toward justice, redemption, and reconciliation—marks of a healthy community. God is the source of both judgment and forgiveness.

All this is rooted in a deep biblical conviction that the essential nature of God is steadfast love, as in the refrain of Psalm 136 that says, "O give thanks to the LORD, for he is good, for his steadfast love endures forever." The Hebrew word in this expression is *hesed*, which expresses God's steadfast love, compassion, and grace.

The Bible is monotheistic in a world that has generally been polytheistic. "Judaism was the first tradition to teach monotheism, the belief that there's only one God. As Judaism evolved, the idea of God evolved, too, focusing on one unknowable, universal, image-less Being, Who, because the universe is framed in Love, requires justice of human beings."[4]

The way the ancient people approached various gods is reflected in Moses' question at the burning bush, when he asks, "If I come to the Israelites and say to them, 'The God of your ancestors has sent me to you,' and they ask me, 'What is his name?' what shall I say to them?" (Exodus 3:13).

Moses asks for God's "handle." The name God reveals to Moses is *YHWH* (3:14-15). This is translated *I AM*, *I AM WHO I AM*, or *I WILL BE WHAT I WILL BE*. The Hebrew may also mean the one who "causes to be."[5] God is nameless, that is, transcendent and beyond all naming. God answers, in essence, "I do not have a handle." In the ancient world, people believed that if the right deity was named and the right sacrifice offered, one could secure a good crop, many offspring, success in war, etc. However, the God of Abraham, Isaac, and Jacob is different. The sovereign Creator of the universe cannot be manipulated.

When Jewish readers come to the Hebrew word *YHWH* in the Hebrew text, they substitute, out of reverence and respect, the words "the LORD." Some versions of the Bible, such as the New Revised Standard Version, capitalize the word "LORD" to indicate that the Hebrew word is being translated. Ironically, *YHWH*, which means "no name," has become the word *Yahweh*, a name for the Deity.

> If you chose a verb or an action to "name" God, what would it be? As a group, make a list of verbs that could "name" God.

Interestingly, this I AM word, *YHWH*, is not a noun, but a verb.[6] The Bible understands God to be active, more like a verb than a noun. One can give a name to a static object like an idol, but the living God cannot have a name because God is not a thing.[7] The Hebrew Bible has many prohibitions against making any kind of representation of God. The commandment against taking God's name in vain expresses a profound understanding that even conversation about God runs the risk of idolatry. In Jewish tradition, it is appropriate to talk to God in prayer but not to talk about God.[8]

God is active in human history, even among those who are not Israelites. In Isaiah 45:1-6, God appoints King Cyrus, as

> In 1879, at Nineveh, a team led by Assyrian archaeologist Hormuzd Rassam found a clay cylinder with an Akkadian language inscription of the edict mentioned in Ezra 1:1-4. The cylinder is housed in the British Museum.[9]

"his anointed" (that is, *messiah*), to liberate the Israelites from captivity in Babylon. Ezra 1:1-7 describes how Cyrus supported the rebuilding of the Temple in Jerusalem and quotes an edict by Cyrus that was distributed throughout his empire. In this edict, King Cyrus refers to "the LORD, the God of heaven," thus affirming monotheism. Yet, the edict reverts to a polytheistic, localized-god motif when it refers to "the God of Israel—he is the God who is in Jerusalem." So, it isn't necessary to have a full understanding of God to be used by God!

The first five books of the Bible are called the Torah, the law (or teaching) of Moses. The Torah includes a unique list of instructions, sometimes called the *Decalogue*, or "Ten Words" (Exodus 20:1-17). Many tend to regard the Ten Commandments as a list of rules; however, the commandments also offer insight into the nature of God, the relationship between God and the community, and how God's people should relate to one another. The first three commandments are about God. The fourth is about the sabbath. The final six are about living respectfully with others. Taken together, they provide important insight into what it means to be the people of God.

> Read the Ten Commandments in Exodus 20:1-17. What insight do you gain into God? Into God's relationship with the people? Into God's expectations for the people?

> The Ten Commandments are found in Exodus 20:1-17:
>
> *You shall have no other gods before me;*
> *You shall not make for yourself an idol;*
> *You shall not make wrongful use of the name of the LORD your God;*
> *Remember the sabbath day, and keep it holy;*
> *Honor your father and your mother;*
> *You shall not murder;*
> *You shall not commit adultery;*
> *You shall not steal;*
> *You shall not bear false witness against your neighbor;*
> *You shall not covet.*

In the ancient world, gods were generally feared. The Bible sometimes portrays God as One to be feared, but the dominant biblical view of God is one of respect or awe. The Bible sees the implications of human sin and injustice as signs of God's judgment. But, the Bible also understands God to be compassionate toward creation, particularly toward the oppressed. Grace, the undeserved forgiveness of God, is the distinctive quality that sets the God of Israel apart from the various gods of antiquity. We see this grace expressed in Exodus 34:6-7 and restated in Psalm 145:8-9, which says, "The LORD is gracious and merciful, slow to anger and abounding in steadfast love. The LORD is good to all, and his compassion is over all that he has made."

> Read Exodus 34:6-9 and Psalm 145:8-9. How do these Scriptures inform your understanding of God's grace and mercy? How do you experience God's compassion, grace, and mercy in your life? How do you see God's grace at work in the world?

God's concern for the oppressed inspired prophets to speak a corrective word to those in power. The prophet Nathan confronted King David's injustice against Uriah (2 Samuel 11–12 and Psalm 51). The prophet Elijah confronted King Ahab's idolatry (1 Kings 18:17-18). And the prophet Amos confronted King Jeroboam II and the leaders of Israel for their mistreatment of the poor (Amos 5:21-24).

> Read 2 Samuel 11–12, Psalm 51, 1 Kings 18:17-18, and Amos 5:21-24. How do the prophets present the understanding of God's grace, mercy, and compassion? How do they present God's judgment? What insight do you gain into God's nature from these Scriptures?

What Does the Bible Say About Jesus?

From the earliest times, Isaiah 53:3-9, part of one of the so-called "servant songs" (Isaiah 42:1-4; 49:1-6; 50:4-9; 52:13–53:12), has been very important to the Christian tradition as a way to understand God's work through Jesus Christ. Verses 3 and 5 from this Scripture tell us that "[Jesus] was despised and rejected by others; a man of suffering.... He was wounded for our transgressions, crushed for our iniquities; upon him was the punishment that made us whole, and by his bruises we are healed." This Scripture brings to my mind a stream of images: Lincoln's funeral train, John Kennedy's funeral procession, New York Fire Department personnel running into the twin towers in a valiant attempt to save others, the gruesome scourging scene in Mel Gibson's *The Passion of the Christ*, and a Peter Marshall sermon I once heard on audio tape called, "Were You There When They Crucified My Lord?" Many churches read this Scripture from Isaiah on Good Friday. As a Christian, I cannot read it without thinking about Jesus. Faithful readers of the Bible also see other interpretive possibilities: the prophet himself, someone the prophet knew, or perhaps the Jewish people as a whole.

Theologians call suffering for the sake of others "substitutionary atonement." It is rooted in the Jewish understanding of sacrifice, an offering that somehow makes things right with God. I respect the doctrine of substitutionary atonement because it has had profound meaning for countless people through the ages. Some modern Christians have difficulty with this doctrine because it seems barbaric that God would send Jesus on a death mission, and I respect their honest questioning of this traditional doctrine. For me, the power of Isaiah 53 does not lie solely in that God sent Jesus to die for our sins or that it predicted Jesus, although I respect those who hold this aspect of prophecy dear. I don't read Isaiah 53 as a proof that Jesus is the Messiah. I don't argue with this interpretation; it's just not what makes this passage so powerful for me. For me, the power of Isaiah 53 lies in something so utterly simple that it may be overlooked entirely. I am awed by Isaiah 53 because these words inspired Jesus. Jesus lived into these words. These words shaped the church's understanding of the meaning of Jesus' life and mission.

> Read Isaiah 53:6-9. In what ways does this Scripture inform your understanding of Jesus? How does it challenge you? How does it enrich your faith?

Jesus gave a whole new meaning to the concept of Messiah. For him, it was more than political, although he has changed politics forever.[10] The idea of redemptive suffering—that one could be healed by the suffering of another—was born in the Jewish Exile.[11] This concept, this reality, expressed so eloquently in Isaiah 53 and embodied so completely in Jesus, is at the very heart of who Jesus was, is, and will be. That's what *I* mean when I say, "Jesus died for me!"

The four primary portraits of Jesus are called the Gospels, and are known to us as Matthew, Mark, Luke, and John. While each has its own distinctive focus, from the portraits they present we learn that Jesus was from Nazareth, at that time a tiny village in the Galilean hill country. He was a carpenter by trade, as was his father, Joseph. Jesus was a rabbi, a teacher, who spent time with John the Baptist. Following common rabbinical practice, Jesus gathered some disciples, or students, around him. Three were especially close: Peter, James, and John. There were nine others in the inner circle, known as "the twelve." There were others in his entourage, which seemed to ebb and flow in size.

The New Testament contains episodes in Jesus' life, which focus on a period of about three years when he was in his early thirties. It includes accounts of his travels, his encounters with Jewish leaders and with ordinary people, stories of Jesus healing others, and examples of his teaching. Some saw him as a miracle-worker. Some saw him as a potential king of Israel,

> "God anointed Jesus of Nazareth with the Holy Spirit and with power; ... he went about doing good and healing all who were oppressed by the devil, for God was with him" (Acts 10:38).

one who might lead a revolt against the Roman occupation troops. He was crucified, or put to death by being nailed to a cross. The New Testament gives considerable attention to his arrest and execution. For example, seven of sixteen chapters in the Gospel of Mark deal with the week leading up to the discovery of his empty tomb. The mysterious resurrection of Jesus became the focal point of his followers' proclamation that Jesus was the long-awaited Jewish messiah.

> Which Gospel stories of Jesus' life and ministry have been most meaningful to you in your faith development? Why?

A brief summary of the Jesus story is found in Peter's sermon at Caesarea Philippi given at the house of Cornelius, a Roman centurion (Acts 10:34-44). Some churches read these verses on Easter, the annual celebration of Jesus' resurrection. This sermon tells how God used Jesus to do good and to heal. Peter and the other followers of Jesus had experienced forgiveness and had become a community where the forgiveness of others was practiced in the name of Jesus. The followers of Jesus described in the New Testament were convinced that Jesus had been raised from death by God and that somehow the presence of Jesus continued to be with them, not in body but in spirit. These followers were also convinced that they, like Jesus, would experience resurrection and have eternal life with God.

> Read Acts 10:34-44. How does Peter's sermon speak to your understanding of Jesus? What aspect of Peter's sermon means most to you as you consider your faith?

One way to explore what the Bible says about Jesus is to consider some of the names, or titles, the New Testament writers give for Jesus. The name *Jesus* is a form of Joshua, which means "God saves." The early church understood Jesus as the new Moses, so it was quite appropriate that he would be named after Moses' successor, Joshua.

Matthew 1:23 quotes Isaiah 7:14 in saying, " 'they shall name him *Emmanuel*,' which means, 'God is with us' " (italics added). The New Testament affirms that God is somehow fully present, or incarnate, in Jesus. Not only is God present with us, but God communicates with us, providing compassion, direction, and constructive criticism.

"And the Word became flesh and lived among us." Here, John 1:14 calls Jesus the **Word**. Christians understand Jesus to be the incarnate Word of God, who was once in human form and whose Spirit is present with us still.

Christians believe Jesus is *Messiah* (in the Hebrew), or *Christ* (in the Greek), which means "the Anointed One." Christ, or messiah, is a title, first used for the king of Israel, referring to the practice of anointing, or pouring olive oil on the new king as a sign of God's presence with the king and with the people ruled by the king. *King* and *Lord* are other names for Jesus, as in "King of kings and Lord of lords" (1 Timothy 6:15). We call Jesus the *Son of God*, a messianic title denoting the special relationship between God and Jesus. For some, perhaps most, Christians, this title refers to Jesus' divinity, as in God's only son.

Look through the New Testament or a hymnal for names and titles given to Jesus, such as **Prince of Peace**, **Savior**, **Master**, **Friend**, and **Hope**. What name or title for Jesus is most meaningful to you? Why?

Sometimes Jesus is referred to as the *Son of Man*, a rich Old Testament term, which sometimes refers to ordinary humans or to the coming judge at the end of time. The early church seems to have combined the traditional Jewish view of a political messiah—as in Jesus, the *King of the Jews*—with the apocalyptic hope of a cosmic, end-of-time savior, that is, the Son of Man.

Paul, Jesus' most influential follower, became a disciple after Jesus' death and resurrection. Some of Paul's letters are included in the New Testament and have had a profound impact on later generations' understandings of Jesus. Philippians 2:5-11, likened to a hymn because of its poetic and rhythmic qualities, succinctly expresses the early church's understanding of Jesus as servant, as one who "emptied himself" and "humbled himself." God honored, or exalted, Jesus for his self-giving nature. Thus, Jesus is worthy of a bow from every knee and recognition from every tongue that he is Lord.[12]

The letter to the Ephesians seems to summarize Paul's understanding of Jesus. Scholars think this likely was either Paul's last known letter or a letter written posthumously by one of his followers. It soars with cosmic implications. Jesus shapes our understanding of ourselves, the community of faith, and the world. Our faith and our very lives are summed up in Jesus. A paraphrase of Ephesians 1:7-10 in *The Message* offers a contemporary interpretation of this Scripture:

> Because of the sacrifice of the Messiah, his blood poured out on the altar of the Cross, we're a free people—free of penalties and punishments chalked up by all our misdeeds. And not just barely free, either. *Abundantly free!* He thought of everything, provided for everything we could possibly need, letting us in on the plans he took such delight in making. He set it all out before us in Christ, a long-range plan in which everything would be brought together and summed up in him, everything in deepest heaven, everything on planet earth. (Ephesians 1:7-10)

In the New Testament, salvation, or wholeness, comes through aligning ourselves with Jesus. "In Christ God was reconciling the world to himself …" (2 Corinthians 5:19). In the New Testament, God makes things right between God and humanity through Jesus. Jesus is a model for our relationship with God—grounded in prayer, focused on finding and living out God's will, and confident in our ultimate union with God through resurrection and eternal life. Jesus is a model for our relationships with others—grounded in compassion, honest, ready to make amends, and committed to justice. For Christians, *everything* in heaven and on earth is brought together and

> Read Ephesians 1:7-10 in several versions or translations of the Bible (NIV, NRSV, KJV, for example). Which version means most to you? Why?

summed up in Jesus. As we trust Jesus, put our complete confidence in him, and align our lives after him as our model for how to live, we experience freedom. We are abundantly free. Jesus gives us the freedom to put others first and to do no harm. God's grace, through Jesus, brings a freedom that is tender, not arrogant.

How do you understand salvation? Wholeness? Grace?
Freedom? How does Jesus
offer these in your life?

What Does the Bible Say About the Holy Spirit?

Christians are monotheists. We believe in one God, Creator of all things and sovereign over all things. Christians inherited this monotheistic understanding from Judaism, and we share it with our younger sibling, Islam. Jews, Christians, and Muslims are monotheists.

The New Testament describes how people encountered God through Jesus. Christians believe Jesus was a manifestation of God made "flesh," as it says in John 1:14. Colossians 1:15 describes Jesus as the visible "image of the invisible God." The affirmation of Jesus as both human and divine sets Christianity apart from Judaism and Islam. Judaism sees Jesus as a great rabbi. Islam views him as a great prophet. Neither sees Jesus as "Son of God" or divine.

Judaism, Christianity, and Islam all understand God to be *spirit*. All three understand this Spirit to be *holy*. Christianity understands God's Spirit, or the Holy Spirit, as one of the three Persons of the triune God. Christians believe that after Jesus' earthly life ended on the cross, and after his mysterious reappearance, his *resurrection*, another manifestation of God's presence was experienced by the early church. This presence continues to be experienced in the church today.

In the Bible, the words translated "spirit" can have many meanings. Spirit can mean "wind" or "breath." It can also be understood as the power of God that creates (Genesis 1:2), that is given to Israel's heroes (Judges 14:6), that inspires rulers (1 Samuel 16:13; Isaiah 11:2), and that inspires prophets (Zechariah 7:12). These understandings develop further in the New Testament. The power of the Holy Spirit is associated with Mary and the birth of Jesus (Luke 1:35). John the Baptist is filled with the Holy Spirit even before his birth (Luke 1:15). The Holy Spirit rests on Simeon who recognizes the infant Jesus as the Messiah (Luke 2:25). Jesus' baptism initiates his ministry in the power of God's Holy Spirit (Matthew 3:16; Mark 1:10; Luke 3:21-22; John 1:31-34). Jesus' healing power comes through the Holy Spirit (Matthew 12:22-32). The Holy Spirit is the supreme gift to those who ask in prayer (Luke 11:13) and is promised to the disciples (Luke 24:49). The Holy Spirit is understood as a Comforter, Advocate, or Counselor sent in Jesus' name to remind Jesus' followers of the things he said and to teach them "everything"

(John 14:26). In a post-resurrection appearance, Jesus "breathes" the Holy Spirit on his followers (John 20:22). The Holy Spirit empowers the birth of the church at the Jewish festival of Pentecost (Acts 2). In the writings of Paul, the presence of the Holy Spirit defines the life of the new community of faith, which has a "new life of the Spirit" (Romans 7:6). The proof or "fruit" of the presence of the Holy Spirit is demonstrated through "love, joy, peace, patience, kindness, generosity, faithfulness, gentleness, and self-control" (Galatians 5:22-23).

> Find a favorite hymn about the Holy Spirit in your church hymnal. Why is it your favorite? What does it say to you about God's presence and power?

Thus, the Holy Spirit is our connecting link with the Creator of the universe, whom Christians traditionally have called "Father," and with the historical Jesus. The Holy Spirit empowers our life together as God's people.

Some Christians give strong emphasis to the Holy Spirit. The Holiness tradition of Christianity believes that after a person is saved, or receives salvation and becomes a Christian, he or she may later receive a second work of grace and be filled with the Holy Spirit. Some of these Christians maintain that once a person has received the Holy Spirit—that is, been baptized by the Holy Spirit or sanctified—the person becomes sinless. The Pentecostal tradition goes one step further by saying that the evidence that one is filled with the Holy Spirit is the gift of speaking in tongues, as mentioned in 1 Corinthians 12–14.

What all Christians have in common is the understanding that the power and presence of God is with us in the Holy Spirit. However you interpret God's presence as Holy Spirit, the Bible gives ample witness to it.

Concluding Remarks

As we explore the Bible for a greater understanding of God's nature, it becomes very clear that the Bible is our primary source. Whether we gain our understanding from worship, from hymns, from Christian education, from devoted Christians, or from other sources, ultimately, our understandings are rooted in the Bible.

> **Closing**
> Read aloud 2 Corinthians 5:17-18: "So if anyone is in Christ, there is a new creation: everything old has passed away; see, everything has become new! All this is from God, who reconciled us to himself through Christ, and has given us the ministry of reconciliation." How does this compare with your experience of being *in Christ*?
>
> Pray the following closing prayer together: God, may Christ live in us, and may we live by faith in Christ. Empower us with your Holy Spirit. Make us new creatures, reconciled with you and offering reconciliation to others. Amen.

Notes

[1] The dates used in this study are from the study manual of DISCIPLE: BECOMING DISCIPLES THROUGH BIBLE STUDY, second edition (Abingdon Press, 1993); page 105.

[2] See the DISCIPLE: BECOMING DISCIPLES THROUGH BIBLE STUDY video presentation "Session One: The Biblical Word," presented by Dr. Albert Outler and Richard B. Wilke.

[3] See Genesis 12:2-3 and Jeremiah 31:31-34.

[4] *Judaism for Dummies*, by Rabbi Ted Falcon and David Blatner, (Hungry Minds, Inc., 2001); page 22.

[5] See the footnotes associated with Exodus 3:13-15 in *The New Oxford Annotated Bible*, third edition, edited by Michael D. Coogan (Oxford University Press, 2001); page 87 HB.

[6] *God Is a Verb: Kabbalah and the Practice of Mystical Judaism*, by Rabbi David A. Cooper (Riverhead Books, 1997); pages 69–71.

[7] See *You Shall Be As Gods: A Radical Interpretation of the Old Testament and Its Tradition*, by Erich Fromm (Fawcett Premier Books, 1966); pages 26–27.

[8] *You Shall Be As Gods*; pages 36–37.

[9] *The Learning Bible*, Contemporary English Version (American Bible Society, 2000); page 839.

[10] At his baptism, as recorded in Matthew 3:17, Jesus heard Psalm 2:7, music sung at the anointing of a new king, and Isaiah 42:1, from the first "servant song." This is like hearing a medley of "Hail to the Chief" and "We Shall Overcome."

[11] From the DISCIPLE: BECOMING DISCIPLES THROUGH BIBLE STUDY video presentation "Session 12: God Restores the People," presented by Walter Brueggemann.

[12] For more information about this Scripture, see "The Letter to the Philippians," in *The New Interpreter's Bible*, Vol. XI (Abingdon Press, 2001); pages 501–10.

CHAPTER 4
WHAT DOES THE BIBLE SAY TO US ABOUT WHAT IT MEANS TO BE HUMAN?

Focus: This session explores what the Bible teaches about both human failure and human potential in light of God's grace.

Gathering

Say in unison the closing words of "A Statement of Faith of the United Church of Canada":

> In life, in death, in life beyond death,
> God is with us.
> We are not alone.
> Thanks be to God.[1]

How do these words speak to you about human failure and human potential?

Pray in unison these words from Augustine's *Confessions*:

> You arouse [us] to take joy in praising you,
> for you have made us for yourself,
> and our heart is restless until it rests in you.
> Amen.[2]

Community

The previous session dealt with what the Bible says about God, Jesus, and the Holy Spirit. *Christian Believer: Knowing God With Heart and Mind* is a 30-week study of major Christian beliefs. Chapter 19, entitled "The Mystery and Message of the Trinity," was, for me, the best chapter in the book and contained this most helpful paragraph:

> In this highly individualistic culture, we need a true understanding of personhood.... The Trinity reveals the divine nature not in individualism (which would, of course, give us three gods) but in relationship and community. When we sing, "God in three persons, blessed Trinity," we declare that one cannot really be a person except in community.... The Holy Trinity ... gives us an eternal paradigm for personhood.[3]

The Bible says the nature of God is communal. We humans are in community with God and with one another. We have been created for God and for one another. God convenes the community, and we are invited. God does not create "lone rangers." God creates us to be part of a holy communion. This message is consistent throughout the Bible, and it reminds us that we are not alone. God is with us. There are times when we *feel* alone, as expressed in Psalm 88:14: "O LORD, why do you cast me off? Why do you hide your face from me?" There are times we think we would prefer not to be in God's presence, as in Jonah 1:2-3: " 'Go at once to Nineveh,'... But Jonah set out to flee to Tarshish from the presence of the LORD." Whether we feel it or not, God is with us, as stated in Psalm 139:7-8: "Where can I go from your spirit? Or where can I flee from your presence? If I ascend to heaven, you are there; if I make my bed in Sheol, you are there."

> When have you, like the psalmist, felt or thought that God was not with you? Have you, like Jonah, felt the need to run away from God? Explain. Read aloud Psalm 139:7-8. What comfort does this Scripture offer?

Solitude and Community

Henri Nouwen's book, *Reaching Out*, describes the movement from loneliness to solitude as a key movement in spiritual growth.[4] The feeling of loneliness is part of the human experience. For some, it is an occasional feeling. For others, loneliness is an ongoing experience. Nouwen's point, and part of the biblical message, is that even when we feel alone, we are in God's presence. If we practice being in the presence of God, our loneliness can be transformed into solitude—a sense of being at peace and at home in God's presence. At the same time, the Bible views community as God's gift. Being human means recognizing the gift of community. We are loved. We are included. Everyone is unique and vital in God's eyes. We are called to view ourselves and others with God's view, to see others as cherished and valued. When we claim this perspective for ourselves and others, we grow spiritually as individuals and communities.

> Do you prefer to be alone or with people? How do you see yourself, as an introvert or an extrovert? How do you understand the movement from loneliness to solitude? How can this movement enrich the times when people are together?

Gratitude

The Bible understands that being human and in relation with the Creator of the universe means living with gratitude. This is majestic and mind-boggling, as reflected in Psalm 139:17-18: "How weighty to me are your thoughts, O God! How vast is the sum of them! I try to count them—they are more than the sand; I come to the end—I am still with you."

We live with gratitude in spite of life's pain. In 1 Thessalonians, Paul writes, "Rejoice always, pray without ceasing, give thanks in all circumstances; for this is the will of God in Christ Jesus for you" (5:16-18). Tragic events such as the September 11, 2001 happenings challenge such a notion. How can we live in gratitude when such horror exists? Our anger is genuine. Our fear is real. As Psalm 139:19 shows, the Bible does not hide from this side of the human experience: "O that you would kill the wicked, O God, and that the bloodthirsty would depart from me." However, the Bible offers God's hope in the midst of such tragedy. Evil will one day be ultimately and finally replaced with God's healing and redemptive judgment.

> Read 1 Thessalonians 5:16-18. How does this Scripture challenge you? How do you think one lives in gratitude in the midst of great tragedy?

I'm not sure I would want to spend a long vacation with Qohelet, the writer of Ecclesiastes.[5] The writings in Ecclesiastes have always seemed to reflect a sour fatalism, with a beginning such as, "Vanity of vanities.... All is vanity" (Ecclesiastes 1:2). But, the years have given me a greater appreciation of the book. This is what the writer of Ecclesiastes says about what it means to be human:

> This is what I have seen to be good: it is fitting to eat and drink and find enjoyment in all the toil with which one toils under the sun the few days of the life God gives us; for this is our lot. Likewise all to whom God gives wealth and possessions and whom he enables to enjoy them, and to accept their lot and find enjoyment in their toil—this is the gift of God. For they will scarcely brood over the days of their lives, because God keeps them occupied with the joy of their hearts. (Ecclesiastes 5:18-20)

The Bible views human life as an extraordinary gift. The understanding of this gift comes through even from the one who wrote "vanity of vanities." Qohelet is able to say that—in spite of life's vanities and disappointments, and in the face of earthly life's fleeting, temporary nature—life is God's gift. The appropriate human response to this gift is very simple and very profound: gratitude. We are invited to live a grateful, thankful life.

> Read Ecclesiastes 5:18-20 in *The Message*. How do you respond to this contemporary paraphrase? How does it inform or challenge your understanding of life as God's gift? Of gratitude as a way of life?

One Thursday I once spoke with a father who was seeing his child through a difficult medical crisis. I asked, "How are you?" He said, "I'm praying for Thursday. Just get us through Thursday." He had learned to pray for strength for that day. Sometimes crisis helps us discover the wisdom of the ages that is expressed in Ecclesiastes 5:20—to take life *one day at a time*. Maybe that's what the writer of Psalm 118:24 had in mind with these words: "This is the day that the LORD has made; let us rejoice and be glad in it."

Human Failure

The Bible recognizes that life is not easy, even life lived in a devoted faith community. Community can be a great joy, and it can be a painful experience. Part of the message of the Bible's story of Adam and Eve is that we humans have had difficulty living in community from the very beginning. The first family couldn't stick to the rules, and rule-breaking is a universal phenomenon (Genesis 3). The first children couldn't get along. Cain killed Abel over bad feelings resulting from a religious offering. The Bible insists that God is intimately involved in the human community. When Cain killed Abel, Abel's blood cried out to God from the ground (Genesis 4:1-15).

God engages the human community by offering structure and boundaries concerning what is right and wrong, proper and improper, ethical and unethical. The Ten Commandments and various "statutes and ordinances" defined the relationship with God and with others. The preamble of the Ten Commandments states the communal nature of God's enterprise with us: "I am the LORD your God, who ... brought you out of the house of slavery."[6] The Bible attributes the very existence of the Israelites to God's act of delivering them from slavery in Egypt. The wilderness experience was marked by God's gracious provision. God offers companionship and guidance, such as when "the LORD went in front of them in a pillar of cloud by day, to lead them along the way, and in a pillar of fire by night, to give them light, so

> How are you now experiencing the journey from bondage to freedom? In what ways are you, as an individual or as a community, still a "work in progress" like the people of Israel in the wilderness?

that they might travel by day and by night" (Exodus 13:21). God provides sustenance, for the "Israelites ate manna forty years, until they came to a habitable land; they ate manna, until they came to the border of the land of Canaan" (Exodus 16:35). Yet, the Israelites complained. "The whole congregation of the Israelites complained against Moses and Aaron in the wilderness" (Exodus 16:2). In spite of the complaints and the disobedience of the Israelites, God never abandoned them. Instead, God gave them the gift of the Law and shaped them into God's people.

Just as God remained with and shaped the people of Israel through their failures, sinfulness, and brokenness, God remains with and shapes us through our failures, our sinfulness, and our brokenness. The Bible says that being human means living with an awareness of sin and brokenness in our individual lives and in our life together as a community. For biblical people, the experience of slavery in Egypt became a metaphor for understanding other struggles in life. Psalm 7 offers prayers for deliverance from personal

> Form three teams. Team One, read Psalm 7. Team Two, read Psalm 38. Team Three, read Psalm 44. In your team, discuss how the psalm addresses a contemporary need for God's saving power and guidance. Share the highlights of your discussion with the entire group.

enemies. Psalm 38 offers prayers for healing. Psalm 44 offers prayers for deliverance from national enemies. Yet, all three of these psalms speak the contemporary need for God's saving power and guidance.

We often forget our identity as grateful people of faith. We often fail. But, the potential of an individual or the human family is not measured by our forgetfulness or our failure. It is measured by our remembrance and by the Resurrection—God's victory over sin and death.

Human Suffering

The opening words of the New Testament letter we know as 1 Peter seem to reflect the dispersion of the Jews after the Romans crushed the Jewish revolt of A.D. 66–70: "Peter, an apostle of Jesus Christ, to the exiles of the Dispersion . . ." The letter is addressed to scattered Christians who are suffering persecution. "Therefore, let those suffering in accordance with God's will entrust themselves to a faithful Creator, while continuing to do good" (1 Peter 4:19). The phrase, "suffering in accordance with God's will," may cause us to wince. Does *God* throw us into the fire or the lion's den? Is it *God's will* that we suffer?

> Read 1 Peter 4:19. What do you believe about suffering and God's will? How do you answer the question, "Is it God's will that we suffer?" Explain your response. How does the Bible inform your understanding?

Whenever I find myself asking this sort of question, I turn to Eugene Peterson for a "second opinion." Sometimes his paraphrase of the Bible, *The Message*, helps me. His take on 1 Peter 4:19 is this: "So if you find life difficult because you're doing what God said, take it in stride. Trust him. He knows what he's doing, and he'll keep on doing it."

The Old Testament writers have no qualms about saying God brings suffering upon the Israelites for punishment or for correction, but when one considers the whole weight of Scripture, it seems clear that suffering means neither that God has *willed* us to suffer nor that God has *abandoned* us. Joseph was sold into slavery by his brothers, and he bloomed where he was planted. The Israelites found themselves in exile in Babylon, but the prophet Ezekiel, who was there, and the prophet Jeremiah, who wrote to the exiles from Egypt, encouraged the Israelites to trust that the Creator would be with them in their suffering.

Sometimes suffering is part of the natural flow of events. Physical pain can be a good thing because it is the body's way of signaling that something is wrong and action is needed. Persons who are numbed to pain for whatever reason may not react to burns or cuts. Sometimes suffering is the result of surprises by natural events such as earthquakes or storms. Sometimes suffering is the result of human error or human malice.

Suffering need not be an occasion for despair. Suffering is something we can work through and get beyond. I once heard Martin Luther King, Sr., the father of Dr. Martin Luther King, Jr., give a sermon on "And It Came to Pass." His point was that time heals and God redeems. Suffering doesn't last forever. Both his son and his wife had been killed by assassins, yet he shared his experience that suffering passes. He entrusted himself to his Creator. So can we. The Bible is very honest about what it means to be human. It does not try to hide from pain. It recognizes that suffering is part of the human experience. But, the Bible consistently

> How has God supported you or someone you know during a time of suffering?

affirms that God will redeem history as well as those who follow God.

God's Grace

The Bible says that being human means living in a *covenant* relationship with God. A covenant is a God-initiated agreement, a divine contract, a relationship of grace and choice.

A consistent thread in the biblical understanding of covenant is that while humanity is notorious for breaking the covenant commitment, God is steadfast. We cannot always be counted on, but we can always count on God. The biblical covenants beginning with Noah and Abraham, finding full expression in Jesus Christ, are rooted in God's grace. God takes the initiative to offer us a relationship of trust based not on our potential or fidelity, but on God's love that is undeservedly steadfast. Our covenant relationship with God is an expression of God's grace.

Joshua 24 describes a covenant renewal scene at Shechem. The people entered into a covenant with God through their leader Moses. Moses had died, and Joshua was their new leader. From time to time, the people of Israel, like us, needed to be brought back to their covenantal intentions. They, like us, needed to be reminded of their identity. Joshua puts the choice before Israel. The Bible understands covenant as something we are invited to share. It is not coercive. It is optional. We are free beings. God invites, but the choice is ours whether or not to respond with fidelity.

> "Now if you are unwilling to serve the LORD, choose this day whom you will serve, whether the gods your ancestors served in the region beyond the River or the gods of the Amorites in whose land you are living; but as for me and my household, we will serve the LORD." —Joshua 24:15

Think for a moment of all the ways in which our lives are surrounded by God's grace. In Romans 5:1-5, Paul talks about God's invitation for us to join in the covenant of Christ. Receiving this covenant means entering into a "sphere of God's grace" in which we now stand (5:2, NEB). We can count on God's undeserved, steadfast love, which we call grace, all our lives and through eternity. We are not always aware of this grace. We do not always appreciate it. We may refuse to acknowledge or receive it. But God's grace is ever-present.

> Make a list of some of the ways in which your life is surrounded by God's grace.

We are people of choice. Perhaps the most basic, most fundamental, most rudimentary choice we make in life is our response to God's grace. This is what Joshua addressed in Joshua 24. Our most appropriate response to this grace is gratitude. Our faith can be duty-bound or gratitude-based. In Paul's life, we witness his transformation from a person motivated by duty to a person of gratitude. Joshua put the choice in terms of *whom will you serve?* Another way to phrase the covenant invitation is this: Will your life be shaped by the "oughts" of duty, which the various gods of the world like to lay on us, or by the energizing power of gratitude?

Paul Tillich writes about human ambiguity. He describes our human failures and our human limitations, yet in spite of these, Tillich affirms that we experience God's Spirit and God's love. He describes the brokenness and imperfect nature of the church, yet in the midst of its ambiguities, somehow this community experiences and shares the "unambiguous life" that Tillich believes was modeled by Jesus. He understands Jesus to be demonstrating and ushering in the "New Being."[7]

In Mark 8:31, Jesus named a disheartening reality within the key religious institutions of his day. "Then he began to teach them that the Son of Man must undergo great suffering, and be rejected." He demonstrated courage to press on because he was rooted in what Tillich calls "the unambiguous life." Jesus was filled with the Spirit and focused on God's mission. He was the embodiment of *agape*, God's self-giving love. Jesus was the embodiment of

> Read Mark 8:27-35. What does this Scripture say to you about Jesus? About his willingness to suffer? About his courage?

courage, and we, the body of Christ, have been given this courage.

God's grace gives us strength to face whatever pain comes our way. The Bible communicates that part of what it means to be human is to experience the courage of others and to live with courage ourselves. The word "courage" is a cousin to the word "heart." To be encouraged is to be heartened. To be discouraged is to be disheartened. There is much in life that seeks to discourage or dishearten. We might attribute some of these discouraging realities to the devil or to the forces of evil in the world, to human depravity, human nature, or human frailty, or to the random acts of nature such as storms or earthquakes.

God's Will

The Bible affirms that we are the product of God's *intentionality*. We are not accidents or random acts of nature. We were created with a divine intent. God had a purpose in mind for each of us. Leslie Weatherhead expresses this eloquently in his classic book, *The Will of God*. When I experience self-doubt, or when I am down on someone else, it helps me to read Psalm 139 and be reminded of my identity, and the identity of other members of the human family. I am, and we are, "fearfully and wonderfully made" (139:14). The word "fearfully" could be replaced with the word "awesomely," since *fear* in this context implies *awe*. We stand in awe of God's creation. Psalm 139 is one of the great testimonies of life understood as a gift from God. The language is simple, quaint, and yet profound: "You knit me together in my mother's womb" (139:13). "My frame was not hidden from you, when I was being made in secret, intricately woven in the depths of the earth" (139:15). God is the divine knitter, the eternal weaver.

The Bible affirms each person's worth by expressing God's investment in our creation. Psalm 139:16 says, "In your book were written all the days that were formed for me, when none of them as yet existed," which is the Bible's way of saying that God has a stake in our lives, that God is deeply concerned about each of our days. God is the all-knowing Presence who brought us into being and does not abandon us. There is a companion idea in Psalm 116:15, which says, "Precious in the sight of the LORD is the death of his faithful ones." Another translation phrases this verse: "The LORD's loved ones are precious to him; it grieves him when they die" (NLT). God is fully invested and fully involved in our human experience from conception through death and beyond.

> Read Psalm 139. Sketch a picture based upon your reading. Tell one another about what you have sketched and why. Which verses speak most to you? What is your response to the psalm? What does it say to you about God's care for you? For all people?

Human Potential

The biblical understanding of our humanity is rooted in our freedom. We have been set free by God. The Exodus from Egypt stands as the dramatic announcement of this freedom, and there are reminders throughout the Bible of this essential part of our Judeo-Christian identity. In Deuteronomy, the people are called to remember: "The LORD brought us out of Egypt ... he brought us into this place.... So now I bring the first of the fruit of the ground that you, O LORD, have given me"(26:8-10).

> Read Deuteronomy 26:5-10. How does this Scripture apply to your life? How might it inform your own response to God's grace?

The Scripture captures the power of repetition in its use of the word "brought." The people have been "brought" to freedom; thus their offerings are presented to God in an act of freedom and gratitude. The ancient Israelites were taught to recite the litany found in Deuteronomy 26:5-10 when they brought their annual first fruits offering. Because God brought us out of slavery and brought us to this place, we have brought our offering. In a symbolic way, this movement from bondage to freedom in the power and grace of God leads us to the response of gratitude. Our human potential emerges from our willingness to respond with gratitude to God's grace in our lives.

The Bible says part of what it means to be human is to deal with our tendency to be clannish. The Israelites repeatedly segregate themselves from non-Jews, the "Gentiles." But, the Bible also calls the Israelites to be a witness and a blessing for the whole world. In John 4:9, we find one of the most profound questions in Scripture: "How is it that you, a Jew, ask a drink of me, a woman of Samaria?" In what may seem like small talk in a public place, this dialogue between Jesus and the woman at the well offers some clues about what it means to be human. The weight of the biblical message, typified by this vignette, is that God prefers involvement rather than isolation and engagement rather than estrangement. Jesus engaged the Samaritan woman at the well. The early church picked up on this conversation and others like it among the stories of Jesus. The church quickly realized that its mission would not be confined to Judaism, but would engage the whole world.

Two events occurred in 2004 that led me to make a commitment: I will not do anything that is divisive or sectarian. Also, I will seek involvement rather than isolation and engagement rather than withdrawal. The first event was when I viewed *Kathryn: The Story of a Teller*, a feature-length documentary about Kathryn Tucker Windham. This amazing woman has balanced the inward journey of prayer, solitude, and reflection with the outward journey of involvement and engagement. In one scene, Kathryn says that she is trying to start a movement of comb-playing. The camera then cuts away to a scene in her hometown of Selma, Alabama, where an interracial gathering of people make music together with their combs. A white physician, who, along with Kathryn, was on Selma's school board in 1965 and an African American attorney in Selma, describes how, in the words of another interviewee, Kathryn was the thread that held the community together in a difficult time.[8]

The other event was the terrorist bombing of a hotel at Taba, an Egyptian resort on the northern tip of the Red Sea. Six years earlier, in 1998, I was part of a group that spent the night in that hotel on our way from Jerusalem to Saint Catherine's monastery in the Sinai Peninsula. People of all faiths must find ways to talk to one another so there can be a united human effort to shun terrorist action by extremists of *any* religion. No longer will I act or think solely within the bounds of my Christian faith. For me, part of what it means to be human and Christian is to engage in dialogue with people outside the Christian community.

You, too, can discern new dimensions of human potential in your personal life and in your life as a community of faith. Look around you. What do you see and hear in your community? How does your grateful response to God's grace inform your choices? In a life of faith, questions such as these are ongoing. As we work through our failures and recognize God's grace one day at a time, we find ways to respond with gratitude. We offer ourselves to God's vision for human potential.

Closing

Say again in unison the closing words of the "Statement of Faith of the United Church of Canada":

> In life, in death, in life beyond death,
> God is with us.
> We are not alone.
> Thanks be to God.

Pray silently about what this statement says in your life. Close the session with the following prayer: God of life and hope, we thank you for leading us into your freedom. Help us to recognize your grace at work in our lives in spite of our failures. Lead us to new commitments that will help us move into the human potential you offer to us in Jesus Christ. In Christ we pray. Amen.

Notes

[1] To read the "Statement of Faith of the United Church of Canada," see *The United Methodist Hymnal* (883).

[2] *The Confessions of St. Augustine*, translated by John K. Ryan (Doubleday, 1960); page 43.

[3] *Christian Believer: Knowing God With Heart and Mind*, study manual, by J. Ellsworth Kalas (Abingdon Press, 1999); page 193.

[4] *Reaching Out: The Three Movements of the Spiritual Life*, by Henri J.M. Nouwen, (Doubleday, 1975); pages 21–48.

[5] For more about the author, see *The New Oxford Annotated Bible*, third edition, edited by Michael D. Coogan (Oxford University Press, 2001); page 944 HB.

[6] Exodus 20:2. See also the previous discussion of the Ten Commandments in Chapter Three of this book on page 40.

[7] *Systematic Theology*, by Paul Tillich, Vol. 3 (University of Chicago Press, 1967); pages 140–82.

[8] *Kathryn: The Story of a Teller*, directed by Norton Dill, produced by Anne Wheeler (The Documentary Depot and Dill Productions, Inc., 2004).

CHAPTER 5
DO THE BIBLE AND SCIENCE CONFLICT?

Focus: This session explores the tensions many people of faith perceive between biblical stories and the tools of science.

Gathering

Read aloud the following Scripture: "And we know that the Son of God has come and has given us understanding so that we may know him who is true; and we are in him who is true, in his Son Jesus Christ. He is the true God and eternal life."—1 John 5:20

Pray together: Almighty God, source of all truth: Give us discerning hearts and minds to think clearly about the facts before us and to see you as the Power behind all learning, all science, and life itself; through Jesus Christ our Lord, who is the way, the truth, and the life. Amen.

A Look in the Mirror

Before we dive into this topic we first need to take a look in the mirror. Most of us, perhaps almost all of us, who live in the first half of the twenty-first century think *scientifically*. You may have never taken a physics course and you may not think of yourself as a scientific person, but simply by virtue of our geographic and chronological location, we are children of the Enlightenment. We are heirs of the Renaissance. Our ways of thinking and our view of the universe have been shaped by Copernicus, Galileo, Descartes, Newton, Rousseau, and Kant. The person you see in the mirror has a bias toward rational thinking. You have been taught to reason. You think logically, or scientifically.

The person you see in the mirror also thinks *historically*. You may or may not have enjoyed history courses in school. One of my friends says, "I hate history," but he can tell you in great detail the process by which the New York Yankees became the dominant major-league baseball team of the twentieth century. He thinks historically. He has a grasp of how one's place in chronology is impacted by what went before and how it sets the stage for what is to follow. A historical consciousness can be understood as a by-product of the scientific worldview that came out of the Enlightenment. We apply a cause-and-effect mentality to the events of history. Thus, we think historically.

> What are some examples of your scientific thinking? Of your historical thinking?

Our worldview is also shaped by the culture in which we live. If you have ever spent time in another culture, you can identify ways you experienced culture shock. Your ways of thinking and acting were different from the ways people in the other culture thought and acted. If you spend enough time with people of another culture, you will begin to identify ways your worldview differs from the prevailing worldview of that culture.

When we open the Bible, we enter a different culture. The people we encounter in the Bible had not been shaped by Copernicus, Galileo, Descartes, Newton, Rousseau, or Kant. This does not mean biblical people were less intelligent than modern people, just that they operated with a different worldview. One of the most important differences is that the Bible was written long before there was a scientific worldview. The biblical world was more open to wonder and surprise. Reality was not viewed through the rational, historical, everything-is-quantifiable lenses that we use today. In the modern world, we expect everything to make sense, to fit into a scientific understanding of cause-and-effect, and to flow with historical precision. Biblical people had a more open-ended view of the universe.

Sometimes we gain insight about the Bible by engaging other cultures in our modern world. A few years ago I was part of a Volunteer in Mission to Bolivia. I was amazed at how little cultural impact the Spanish conquistadors and their descendents have made among the Aymará people of the Andes. I sensed that the Aymará worldview and ways of thinking perhaps are more akin to that of biblical day than to that of twenty-first-century European or North American culture. The Roman Catholic cathedral at Copacabana, on Lake Titicaca, features an ancient statue of Mary that is greatly venerated by the people of that region as the "patron saint of Bolivia." Our team learned that the native folk religion of the Aymará people focused on the figure of *Pachamama*, "earth mother." It became clear to me that when the Spanish conquistadors brought Roman Catholic Christianity to the Andes, the Aymará devotion to Pachamama was linked to the Virgin Mary. Today, the faith of the people in that culture is a blend of Christianity and the ancient folk devotion to Pachamama.[1]

My VIM trip to Bolivia helped me understand the issues presented in 2 Kings 23, where we read about the interface of biblical faith and indigenous religions in the Old Testament story of King Josiah's reign (640–609 B.C.). In the Old Testament, the "high places" were pagan shrines to other gods. Some rulers of Judah tolerated this diversity of religious expression and others, such as Josiah, abolished the high places, insisting that people worship only Yahweh. As I saw the "high places" devoted to Pachamama, I saw the interface of two religions

> When have you experienced culture shock by spending time in another culture? Perhaps it was on a Volunteer in Mission trip, or as a tourist, or while on a tour of military duty. Share with one another an example of how your way of thinking differed from the ways persons in another culture thought.

and the various ways followers of one religion accommodated to or rejected the faith claims of the other religion.

Do the Bible and Science Conflict?

If one insists on reading the Bible the way one reads a science textbook, then the answer is yes. But this is not really a conflict between the Bible and science. It is a conflict that arises from a particular way of *interpreting* the Bible. If we project onto the Bible our scientific ways of thinking, then there will be apparent conflicts between some of the biblical stories and some of the findings of science.

The Bible and science conflict only when one is unable to step outside the prejudices of a modern scientific worldview. In other words, the Bible and science conflict only when one tries to make the worldview and intentions of the biblical writers conform to one's modern scientific, rational, historical, and cultural prejudices. The conflict occurs only when we demand of the Bible that it perform, or read, like a science textbook. When you stop and think about it, that's a rather haughty or arrogant attitude toward the Bible.

If we think scientifically, rationally, and historically, we tend to project this way of thinking onto the Bible. We thus expect the Bible to reflect our worldview and our way of thinking. This is unfair to, and disrespectful of, the biblical writers. Such an approach to the Bible insists that it be interpreted one way. This is sometimes called a "literal" interpretation and often means it conforms to our scientific, rational, and historical way of viewing reality.

Think about some familiar Bible stories that challenge you because they do not fit your worldview. How does a contemporary scientific or historic worldview inform the story? How does it challenge the story? What could the story say to you if you stepped outside of your worldview? What truths does it communicate to you?

There seems to be a conflict between the Bible and science because readers who have a scientific worldview sometimes misinterpret the Bible's pre-scientific language. For example, the biblical writers assumed the earth was flat. A person in that era might say, "God's love extends to the four corners of the earth." I believe that is a true statement because it is a way of saying God's love extends to all persons. But, it is a *poetic* truth, not a *scientific* truth. The world does not have "corners" in the sense that this phrase would have been used originally.

Galileo (1564–1642) understood that scientific knowledge did not necessarily conflict with biblical faith, but the church hierarchy of his day insisted that the Bible must be approached in the same way one would read a scientific textbook. In his *Letter to the Grand Duchess Christine of Lorraine*, he strongly supported the view of Cardinal Baronius that the "Holy Spirit intended to teach us in the Bible how to go to Heaven, not how the heavens go."[2] Unfortunately, Cardinal Baronius was in the minority. When Galileo tried to assert that Copernicus' theory could be reconciled with Scripture, he encountered opposition from theologians and

church leaders. This is a classic example of how religious leaders sometimes demand that the Bible must be read scientifically and that science
must conform to this interpretation of the Bible.

Over time, we have learned that the earth is a relatively small sphere in
a vast universe populated by occasional spheres of stars and planets. But
our language still reflects this
flat earth perspective when we
speak of the four corners of
the earth or God being *up* in
heaven. If a person in
Australia points up to God in
heaven and a person in Alaska
points up, they would be
pointing in different directions. Our present understanding of the universe makes *up*
and *down* language meaningless as a scientific truth. Our
language seeks to communi-
cate that God is transcendent, but the idea that God is *up there* is poetic
truth, not scientific truth. When the Soviet cosmonaut Yuri Gagarin said
he did not see God in the heavens when he orbited the earth, he missed the
point by giving a literal, or scientific, interpretation upon the Christian
faith claim that God is in heaven. When we speak of God as up in heaven,
we are using a spatial, or geographic, metaphor to describe God's transcendence. Another way of communicating God's transcendence is to
think in terms of present/future. God is in the *future*, calling us from the
present into the future that God intends.[3]

> Recall some poetic images that are used in the Bible to help us think about God. Some of these images are mentioned in Chapter 2: rock (1 Samuel 2:2; Psalm 95:1), mother (Isaiah 66:13), eagle (Deuteronomy 32:11-12), fortress (Psalm 31:3), potter (Isaiah 64:8b), water (Jeremiah 2:13; 17:13; John 4:10-15), and light (Isaiah 60:19-20; 1 John 1:5). What other images help you think about God?

Is the Bible True?

Once in a DISCIPLE Bible study class, we were discussing the material
from the Creation stories in Genesis. In the study, professor B. Davie Napier
calls the Creation story in Genesis 1 a "poem."[4] To that statement, one of the
participants replied, "You mean that's *just* poetry?" I said, "Thank you!
You've just demonstrated our modern prejudice that scientific truth is greater
than poetic truth!" The biblical people were more tuned to poetry. Turn it
around: If we read Genesis 1, or any other biblical text, as *just* science or *just*
history, we may rob the story of its greatest meaning and power.

The same issue has arisen in my conversations with sixth grade confirmation classes. The young people ask about Genesis 1, "Where are the dinosaurs?" My response is to say that we let the scientists try to figure out scientific truth, which basically asks *how* questions, such as how the universe was created or how plant and animal life developed. The Bible focuses primarily on *why* questions, that is, why planet earth was created, why creation is good, or why life on earth is a sacred gift from God. In one of these class discussions, a student asked, "Who created God?" Another student responded, "That's a *how* question!"

> Read Genesis 1 and 2. What are some *how* questions that occur to you? What are some *why* questions? How does this story speak the most meaning to you? How does it inform your learning and growth in faith?

Some people are made uneasy when a literal interpretation is questioned because it seems to be questioning the Bible itself. And some are liberated when they realize there are ways to approach the Bible other than a literal interpretation. The liberation comes when one begins to think poetically as well as scientifically. The liberation comes when one seeks to discover the meaning that the biblical writer intended to communicate. For example, did the writer of Genesis 1 intend to communicate that the earth was created in six 24-hour days? Or, was the writer trying to communicate that God created the universe with loving, caring intentionality and orderliness? North Americans in the early twenty-first century tend to think scientifically, so our minds gravitate to questions about the six 24-hour days. Many modern people go to great lengths to somehow reconcile the biblical "six days" with scientific theories of creation. To do so may miss the point entirely about God's gracious, caring, and intricate creativity.

Can a statement be true without being a fact? The following mathematical symbol helps me when I approach the Bible: Truth>Facts. I was once part of a committee charged with choosing the biblical scenes to be depicted on some stained glass windows for a chapel. The group decided the windows should depict scenes from the life of Jesus, as well as two of his most well-known parables, the parable of the good Samaritan in Luke 10 and the parable of the prodigal son in Luke 15. Jesus began the latter parable with the words, "There was a man with two sons." Was this true? Did he have a particular man in mind? Was this a factual story? If this was *just* a story, does this mean the story is untrue?

Sometimes a story conveys a far greater truth than can be revealed by any fact. James Weldon Johnson's *God's Trombones* is a collection of sermons. One of the sermons is "The Creation," a re-telling of the Creation stories of Genesis 1 and 2. Johnson's sermon begins with God stepping out on space, looking around, and saying, "I'm lonely—I'll make me a world."[5] The sermon continues with variations and specific images that emerge from the stories in Genesis. Johnson seeks

> What do you believe is the most important truth in the Creation stories of Genesis 1 and 2? As you have grown in the Christian faith, has your thinking about the meaning of these stories changed? If so, in what ways?

to elaborate and present the truth in the Genesis stories that applies to all human beings. This goal is different than presenting facts scientifically.

Beyond Creationism

The clash between science and a literal interpretation of the Bible is as old as Copernicus (1473–1543), who first challenged an earth-centered view of the universe by suggesting that the sun is the center of the universe. Copernicus was reluctant to publish his theories, and his work was not widely known until late in his life. Protestants first challenged his theories in the early days of the Protestant Reformation as being anti-biblical. Copernicus' theories met opposition from the Roman Catholic Church after these theories were embraced by Galileo (1564–1642) some seventy years after Copernicus' death.[6]

The United States has been the location of a unique debate regarding the Bible and science. This debate is born of a paradox. On one hand, Christianity has been the dominant religion in the United States. On the other hand, the United States Constitution prohibits the establishment of a state religion. Courts have interpreted this "establishment clause" to prohibit public schools from promoting a particular religion or religious doctrine. Within these court-imposed restraints, some state legislatures have sought to encourage the teaching of the biblical accounts of the Creation in Genesis, while discouraging the teaching of theories of evolution.

The issue of creation and public schools received a great deal of attention in the July 1925 trial of John Scopes, a twenty-four-year-old graduate of the University of Kentucky who taught biology at the Rhea County High School in Dayton, Tennessee. He taught Charles Darwin's theory of evolution, which had been outlawed in 1925 by the Tennessee legislature. The legislature feared this teaching would undermine (a literal interpretation of) the Bible. William Jennings Bryan assisted the prosecution and Clarence Darrow assisted the defense in what became highly publicized as "The Monkey Trial." Scopes was found guilty and fined $100. The Tennessee State Supreme Court overturned the conviction on a technicality. The statute stood untested until the law was repealed by the Tennessee legislature in 1967.[7]

When I was a teenager, my grandfather shared with me his memories of the Scopes trial, which led to a discussion about the interface of scientific theories with the biblical stories of the Creation in Genesis 1 and 2. It was then, many years ago, that I was freed from somehow trying to fit the dinosaurs into a literal interpretation of the Creation stories of the Bible. I learned that the Bible is primarily concerned with the meaning of life (*why* questions), not with scientific or historical accounts (*how* questions).

Find several news articles about creationism, intelligent design, and evolution. Identify the central ideas in the articles. How do these articles connect to issues of biblical interpretation?

There has been a renewed effort in the early part of the twenty-first century to read the Bible as a science textbook. This approach is sometimes called "creationism" or "intelligent design." It is an attempt to present the Creation stories of Genesis as science rather than story. Efforts by religious or political leaders to conform scientific theories to a particular way of interpreting the Bible have generally proven futile, overcome by the free market of scientific thought.

Good science and healthy religion ought to engage one another in lively, fruitful conversation about the meaning of life on planet earth. Here is one an example as a starting point: Albert Einstein (1879–1955) developed a new way of looking at the universe. This theory of relativity postulated that the essence of matter is energy. All things are perpetually in motion. This replaced a more static view of the universe that had been in place since Sir Isaac Newton (1642–1727) developed his theories about gravity.[8] Thus, we could say that the elements of the universe, including humanity, are more verb-like than noun-like. This seems to be in harmony with the discovery made by Moses many years earlier at the burning bush of Exodus 3. God is not an object (a noun)—God is the great "I AM" (more verb-like). In the Bible, idols are nouns (objects) and

God is alive, active (verb-like).[9] Psychotherapist Erich Fromm says Jewish faith focuses on what God *does* and what God requires *us* to do rather than on statements *about* God.[10]

Respectful, fruitful conversation between religion and science is vital for the health and long-term survival of our planet. It may be that this conversation also will enable people of various religions to converse with more civility. Religion and science have perspectives to offer about the common good of human society and planet Earth. Rather than trying to dominate or subdue other religions or scientific theories, we Christians would do well to learn from other disciplines and other faiths in order to find ways of working together.

> How can modern physics, following Einstein's understanding of matter, help us understand the biblical admonition against the worship of static, inactive idols? How can it help us focus on God's action?

Stumbling Blocks

To receive a text as divinely inspired does not automatically mean that it is, without question, historically accurate in every respect. I believe that claiming historical accuracy for the Bible creates an inappropriate obstacle or "stumbling block" for many people. Sometimes the church has demanded that, as a litmus test of sorts for your faithfulness, you must accept the Bible's stories as literal, one hundred percent historically accurate accounts. Then, if you do not agree with this particular interpretation, you are considered unfaithful. However, such an approach distorts what really matters.

I would be sad if you said something like, "I cannot accept that the earth was created in six 24-hour days; therefore I cannot be a believer." Or, "I cannot agree that Moses' wooden staff was literally turned into a live snake and then back to a piece of wood; therefore I cannot be a believer." My response would be, "Someone has put a false stumbling block in front of you. Let me suggest some alternative ways of approaching or interpreting that passage."

An example of an appropriate stumbling block would be the command to have no other gods or idols. Such a command is a real challenge because life presents many temptations to worship gods other than our Creator. Another example of a valid stumbling block is the command to love our neighbor. That is an appropriate faith challenge to put before yourself or the faith community.

I would be sad if you said something like, "I have no desire to give up the worship of other gods or idols; therefore I cannot be a believer." Or, "I have no desire to love my neighbor; therefore I cannot be a believer." But, it would be a different kind of sadness. At least in these assertions you would have made a decision based on some basic issues of faith.

As a Christian, I am convinced that a Christian's faith is most secure not when it is based solely on a particular method of interpretation—literal, liberal, allegorical, or otherwise. Rather, I believe a Christian's faith is most secure when it is based solely on grace, the unmerited love and forgiveness of God that is experienced through a relationship with Jesus Christ. Such a relationship transcends any and every method of biblical interpretation.

Closing
Read aloud Genesis 1:31.

Take a moment to name something that bothers you that seems to be a contradiction between the Bible and science. Now take a moment to identify the meaning for life and faith that this Scripture seeks to affirm.

As a closing prayer, read aloud Psalm 8.

Notes

[1] *Bolivia Handbook: The Travel Guide*, second edition, by Alan Murphy (Footprint Handbooks Ltd, 2000); page 133. To read more about the blend of religions in Bolivia, see *Bolivia*, fourth edition, by Deanna Swaney (Lonely Planet, 2001); page 49. For more about the Andean region, see "Andes Empires," by Virginia Morell, in *National Geographic*, June, 2002; pages 106–129.

[2] *Great Books of the Western World*, edited by Robert Maynard Hutchins, Vol. 28 (Encyclopedia Britannica, Inc., 1952); page 126.

[3] For more on this concept, see *A Spirituality Named Compassion and the Healing of the Global Village, Humpty Dumpty and Us*, by Matthew Fox (Winston Press, 1979); pages 36–67.

[4] See the video presentation "Session Two: The Creating God," presented by B. Davie Napier, in DISCIPLE: BECOMING DISCIPLES THROUGH BIBLE STUDY, second edition (Abingdon Press, 1993).

[5] *God's Trombones: Seven Negro Sermons in Verse*, by James Weldon Johnson (Viking Press, 1955); page 17.

[6] Find more information about Galileo at "The Galileo Project," accessible at: http://galileo.rice.edu.

[7] Read more about the Scopes Trial at: http://www.law.umkc.edu/faculty/projects/ftrials/scopes/scopes.htm.

[8] *A Spirituality Named Compassion and the Healing of the Global Village, Humpty Dumpty and Us*; pages141–45.

[9] *God Is a Verb: Kabbalah and the Practice of Mystical Judaism*, by Rabbi David A. Cooper (Riverhead Books, 1997); pages 69–73.

[10] See *You Shall Be As Gods: A Radical Interpretation of the Old Testament and Its Tradition*, by Erich Fromm (Fawcett Premier Books, 1966); page 36–37.

CHAPTER 6
HOW DOES THE BIBLE
HELP US PRAY AND WORSHIP?

Focus: This session explores how the Bible informs prayer, other spiritual disciplines, and worship.

Gathering
Listen to Pachelbel's Canon or a similar reflective piece of music. As the music plays, close your eyes and call to your mind your favorite depiction of Jesus by an artist. Center your heart and mind on Jesus, and listen for what God would speak to you through the silence. After a few moments of silent prayer, read the following Scripture as a responsive reading:

A litany from Psalm 136:1-3:

O give thanks to the LORD, for he is good, for his steadfast love endures forever.
O give thanks to the God of gods, for his steadfast love endures forever.
O give thanks to the Lord of lords, for his steadfast love endures forever.

Dialogue With God

The biblical writers express various understandings of God and human nature. Yet, there are some consistent themes and common threads. One shared premise is that God, the Creator of the universe, engages humanity and offers us a relationship of undeserved love and grace through Jesus. We believe it is the essence of God's nature to desire communication with humanity. The Bible helps facilitate this divine/human communication, which we call prayer.

We believe God initiated this dialogue through God's action in human history and in our own time and place through the Holy Spirit. The Bible is a companion for each person's individual, relational journey with God, as well as a companion for our faith community's life together with God. The act of reading and interpreting the Bible is profoundly personal and profoundly communal. God invites us, both as individuals and as the human community, to be partners in the sacred dialogue of prayer.

St. Benedict of Nursia (born A.D. 480) developed a guideline for prayer and spiritual living. The Benedictine rhythm of prayer begins with listening to God.[1] The writings of Robert K. Greenleaf (1904–1990) encourage us to develop our potential as *listeners*. Greenleaf believed God continuously raises up prophetic voices throughout human history. The variable has been the community's ability (or lack of ability) to *hear* these prophetic voices.[2]

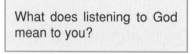

What does listening to God mean to you?

The Bible is a resource to help us listen, meditate upon what we have heard, and formulate our silent or spoken responses to God. Prayer is dialogue between God and humanity. In our relationship with God, and in our prayer dialogue with God, the biblical message indicates that God initiates the relationship and the conversation. Our prayer is a response to God's word first spoken to us. The biblical message reveals that God already knows our innermost thoughts. Thus, we are freed from any need to censor what we say to God. We can freely and fully express ourselves in our prayer dialogue with God. God listens to us better than we listen to God.

Read Exodus 3:1-6. What does this Scripture say to you about God? About Moses? How does this Scripture help you think about prayer as dialogue with God?

The burning bush story in Exodus 3 depicts a dialogue between God and Moses: "When the LORD saw that he had turned aside to see, God called to him out of the bush, 'Moses, Moses!' And he said, 'Here I am'"

(Exodus 3:4). What prepared Moses to notice, to turn aside rather than go on about his business? What cultivated within Moses an attentiveness, an openness, an alertness to God's action in the world? More importantly, how can *we* cultivate a receptivity to God's initiative for engagement in dialogue? The Bible offers some important insights.

Feeling Abandoned

For centuries, people have turned to the Psalms to help find words to pray. One reason the Psalms are so valuable is that every possible human emotion is expressed in them. By eavesdropping on the psalmists' rage, we feel freer to express our anger to God. God is big enough to handle our emotions. By listening to the psalmists express confidence in God's redeeming power, even in the midst of dire crisis, we are encouraged to be hopeful in the midst of *our* dire crises. The Bible helps us learn the vocabulary of prayer—not just the right words to use, but the range of emotions and expectations to bring before God. The psalmists see both anger and compassion in God, judgment and forgiveness, abandonment and redemption. Maybe this was the psalmists' way of saying, "Sometimes we feel abandoned."

In Psalm 66:18-20, the writer believes that if he had harbored iniquity in his heart, God would not have listened: "If I had cherished iniquity in my heart, the Lord would not have listened. But truly God has listened; he has given heed to the words of my prayer. Blessed be God, because he has not rejected my prayer or removed his steadfast love from me." Maybe the psalmist is saying

> Read Psalm 66:16-20. Have you ever felt abandoned? Have you ever wondered if God is listening? How does this psalm address such feelings? How might it inform your times of prayer?

God turns away from unrighteousness, the way a noble person turns away when he or she overhears gossip or demeaning conversation. Perhaps he is saying that iniquity prevents us from responding to God's offer of dialogue, that iniquity cuts off the dialogue. Yet, the psalmist is convinced that God does listen. The psalmist is thankful that God has not rejected his prayer; God has not removed the steadfast love that is at the heart of God's nature.

Asking Questions

Good questions are essential in the learning process. Honest questions build relationships. Respectful questions create community. Healthy questions provide an atmosphere for engagement. Heartfelt questions that express both intellect and emotion form the essence of prayer. The Bible encourages us to present God with our deepest questions: "Answer me, O LORD, for your steadfast love is good; according to your abundant mercy, turn to me. Do not hide your face from your servant, for I am in distress—make haste to answer me" (Psalm 69:16-17).

Psalm 69:16-17 sounds like the poignant conversation between Job and God in Job 38:1–42:6. The Book of Job is itself a question, or an argument, about why bad things sometimes happen to good people. The climax of this questioning comes as God responds to Job's questions by saying, "*I* will question *you*, and *you* shall declare to *me*" (38:3, italics added). At first glance, this may seem like an end to the dialogue, as if God is saying, "Shut up and listen!" However, this is simply an indication of the depth of intimacy, the radical honesty, the probing mutuality going on in this back-and-forth questioning between God and Job. This sort of no-holds-barred questioning continues in the Psalms and Proverbs.

> What questions do you have for God? Have you ever asked, "Why me?" Have you ever been afraid to ask God your deepest, most honest questions? Why? How can the radical honesty in Psalm 69:16-17 help you?

If God didn't love Job (or us) so much, God wouldn't bother to ask such profound questions. On one hand, a reading of Job 38–42 may make it intimidating to ask questions of the Creator of the universe. That's why our questions should be good, honest, respectful, healthy, and heartfelt. But, on the other hand, notice the care God gives in making a response to Job. "Where were you when I laid the foundation for the earth?" (38:4). God, in a sense, puts Job in his place, but this "place" is an intimate, face-to-face encounter with the Almighty.

God cares enough about us to ask us deep questions about our attitudes and our practices. Do we care enough about God to ask our deepest questions? Leander Keck wrote a book years ago called *Taking the Bible Seriously*.[3] Keck, who has the heart of a rabbi/teacher, understands that the best way to read the Bible is to wrestle with it, thus allowing the Bible to become what God intended it to be—a tool for honest dialogue.

Pray Without Ceasing

Paul's words from 1 Thessalonians 5:17, telling us to "pray without ceasing," are tucked inside a paragraph of instruction about life in Christian community. Eugene Peterson's *The Message* paraphrases this as saying to "pray all the time." Peterson provides the heading "The Way He Wants You to Live" at 1 Thessalonians 5:12. This contemporary version of the Bible paraphrases 1 Thessalonians 5:16-21 as follows: "Be cheerful no matter what; pray all the time; thank God no matter what happens. This is the way God wants you who belong to Christ Jesus to live. Don't suppress the Spirit, and don't stifle those who have a word from the Master. On the other hand, don't be gullible. Check out everything, and keep only what's good."

> To get the full context, read 1 Thessalonians 5:12-22 in both *The Message* and in another version, such as the NRSV or NIV. Which version says the most to you? Why? How does the Scripture challenge you?

Did Paul have in mind the people who spend their entire days at the Temple, praying? I think of today's Hasidic Jews, with their continuous presence at the Western Wall of the Temple ruins in Jerusalem. A member of a monastic community once told a group visiting the monastery that the monks' daily mission is to pray for the world. Some people consider prayer to be their vocation. But, Paul seems to have in mind the ordinary people of Thessalonica as they live out their daily lives in the market place. To "pray without ceasing," as the traditional communion liturgy reads, is to move toward making one's very *life* a prayer—to make our lives holy and reasonable sacrifices (or offerings).

John Shelby Spong describes how his prayer life changed from spending an hour a day praying, or talking to God, to spending an hour in silence, prayerfully listening to God, and the rest of his day is then spent living out his prayer. His entire day is prayer. Prayer is action. Prayer is everything Spong does. He seeks to bring an awareness of God's presence into

> How might your attitude about an ordinary, everyday task change if you thought of it as a prayer? What does praying without ceasing mean to you?

everything he does. Spong seeks to be attentive to God and to invite others to be attentive to God in the routine events of daily life.[4] Prayer is empty if it is disconnected from the world and from the realm of human ethics and justice.

The call to "pray without ceasing" has been lived out in Christian history in various ways. One excellent way to pray unceasingly is the "breath prayer," a simple, short prayer that one prays as often as possible. It employs the address you most naturally use in prayer, such as "God," "Father," "Lord," "Jesus," "Master," etc. It focuses on what you identify as your greatest known need at the moment, such as "peace," "joy," "love," "hope," "healing," "strength," etc. A breath prayer could be, "Father, let me feel your joy," or "God, give me peace," or "Jesus, fill me with your love." The primary purpose of a breath prayer is to enhance our attentiveness to God's presence each moment. A short, simple breath prayer can help us pray for other people and other concerns throughout the day. It is a reminder that God is in the process of transforming us and our world at every moment, and it is a way of joining our prayer with the Spirit's intercession for us. "The Spirit helps us in our weakness; for we do not know how to pray as we ought, but that very Spirit intercedes with sighs too deep for words" (Romans 8:26).

The Journey Inward and the Journey Outward

Mark 1:33-35 gives a memorable snapshot of Jesus' prayer life: "the whole city was gathered around the door. And he cured many who were sick with various diseases, and cast out many demons.... In the morning, while it was still very dark, he got up and went out to a deserted place, and there he prayed."

Jesus began his day with prayer. If early morning prayer was a feature of Jesus' life, then perhaps there is a lesson here for *our* living. Jesus' active life was laced with times of solitude. He was constantly involved with multitudes of people, engaged with the pressing issues that were of paramount importance to them: "the whole city was gathered around the door" of the house at Capernaum (Mark 1:33). Jesus was a healing presence for the entire community: "he cured many who were sick with various diseases, and cast out many demons" (1:34). This healing came from a very deep

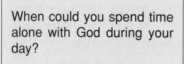

When could you spend time alone with God during your day?

well. Jesus was centered in a life of solitude and prayer. Jesus was intimately connected with God almighty. Divine energy flowed through him to the people who were in need of healing. Jesus' time alone with God energized him for the tasks ahead and enabled him to discern God's direction for his life: "And he went throughout Galilee, proclaiming the message in their synagogues and casting out demons" (1:39). Out of the solitude came clarity. Jesus' life was a rhythmic balance between the journey inward and the journey outward. Engagement followed solitude. Solitude followed engagement.

We do not know the content of Jesus' prayer mentioned in Mark 1:35. The Scripture simply says, "and there he prayed." Jesus' model of prayer seems significantly weighted toward *listening*. Listening seems to be his primary posture of prayer. This raises the question for us, "How much of our praying is listening, and how much is speaking?" Perhaps we too often rush into the speaking dimension of prayer, telling God what we need or what we think God needs to do to heal the world, rather than spending time listening for what we need to do to be participants with God in the healing of our souls and of the planet.

> How does prayer shape the rhythm of your life? How does your life's rhythm reflect the Jesus balance between solitude and engagement, the "journey inward" and the "journey outward?"

Simplicity in Prayer

The Jesus style of prayer is simple and modest. It is not elaborate or showy. A brief section of the Sermon on the Mount in Matthew describes Jesus' style of prayer and fasting (6:5-18). Within this section is the Lord's Prayer, which is prayed countless times each day in many languages. When we look at Matthew 6:5-18, because of its importance to the Christian faith, our eyes are almost immediately drawn to this prayer. Thus, we may too quickly pass over the words that introduce this prayer and the words that follow it. The prayer is launched with a call to simplicity and modesty: "When you are praying, do not heap up empty phrases as the Gentiles do; for they think that they will be heard because of their many words. Do not be like them, for your Father knows what you need before you ask him" (6:7-8). Jesus calls us to pray with focus upon God and what God wants for us. Prayer is rooted in the conviction that God knows best, that God wants what is best for us. Prayer, then, is tuning in to God's yearning for us. Prayer is aligning our will, our yearning, with God's.

We need not worry about mastering "techniques" of prayer. Jesus says that, mechanically, prayer is simple, although the results of our prayer may lead us to difficult paths of service. This reverses a popular view of prayer, which maintains that if you find a secret or magical form, structure, or technique of prayer, then your life will be easy. Jesus teaches us simply to focus our attention and heart on God. The result

> Read Matthew 6:1-8. How do Jesus' teachings help you in your times of prayer?

of this kind of prayer is a changed life, and the transformation involves new values and behaviors and the taming of our desires and appetites. The Jesus style of prayer is simple, not complicated, and puts us in synch with God's way, which Jesus calls the kingdom of God.

The Lord's Prayer is the essence of simplicity and modesty: "Your kingdom come. Your will be done." This couplet, consistent with repetitive restatements throughout the Psalms, provides the simple theological framework for the Lord's Prayer. For our part, the prayer expresses our human needs with utter

> Read the Lord's Prayer in Matthew 6:9-13 and Luke 11:2-4. Write the prayer in your own words. What does it say to you about the connection between prayer and life?

simplicity—we need help with daily bread, forgiveness, and avoiding temptation.

The very brief section about fasting in Matthew 6:16-18 does not provide a primer for how to fast but a short word about one's *style* of fasting. Fasting is not the same as weight loss practices or eating disorders, such as anorexia or bulimia. The spiritual discipline of fasting, a very common practice in Jesus'

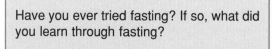

> Have you ever tried fasting? If so, what did you learn through fasting?

day, has the purpose of keeping one's focus on God. Jesus didn't need to tell his disciples how to begin a fast, how long it should be kept, how to break the fast, etc. They knew all of that. He reminded them that the purpose of fasting, as in prayer, is to focus on God. Jesus instructed them to fast with the same kind of simplicity and modesty that we are to bring to prayer.

How Can the Bible Draw Us Together for Worship?

The purpose of prayer and fasting is to stay focused on God. When we join our praying hearts with other hearts that are praying, we have a worshiping community.

> Do not let the foreigner joined to the LORD say, "The LORD will surely separate me from his people;" . . . And the foreigners who join themselves to the LORD, to minister to him, to love the name of the LORD, and to be his servants, all who keep the sabbath, and do not profane it, and hold fast my covenant—these I will bring to my holy mountain, and make them joyful in my house of prayer; their burnt offerings and their sacrifices will be accepted on my altar; for my house shall be called a house of prayer for all peoples. Thus says the Lord GOD, who gathers the outcasts of Israel, I will gather others to them besides those already gathered. (Isaiah 56:3, 6-8)

The "holy mountain" is Jerusalem. The "house of prayer" is the Temple. I find hope for our fragmented world in an excerpt from this biblical passage, which is engraved above an entrance to Temple Emanu-El, a Jewish synagogue in Birmingham, Alabama: "My house shall be a house of prayer for all people."

Anthony was a fourth-century hermit who lived in the Egyptian desert. Pilgrims visited the hut of this "desert father" for prayer and spiritual direction.[5] Benedict of Nursia, a fifth-century monk, provided a "rule" of life for European monastic communities that is still used around the world.[6] The Christian faith made it through tough times during the Middle Ages in large part due to the spiritual vitality that came through two monastic orders. The Franciscans were founded by Giovanni Francesco di Bernadone (1182–1226), commonly known as Saint Francis of Assisi. The Dominicans were founded by Dominic de Guzman (1170–1221), or Saint Dominic.[7] The nucleus of Christianity has been various "houses of prayer," whether huts or cathedrals, founded by a wide assortment of people.

What kind of "house of prayer" would Anthony build today? If Francis and Dominic were alive today, how might their "houses of prayer" look? Imagine a group of Christians, Jews, Muslims, Buddhists, and Hindus living together in the same community, living out their individual faith traditions with a focus of prayer for the world, replete with daily dialogue, prayer and worship. Sound farfetched? In their own time, many people questioned the beliefs of Anthony, Benedict, Dominic, and Francis.

An old friend of mine many years ago said that "psychosis is where there is no *us*, only *them*. Agape love is where there is no *them*, only *us*." Today there are voices in the Christian community speaking against all Muslims, saying, "It's either us or them." I believe we need to speak against extremists who misuse any religion, but the most important action we can take today is to bring people of goodwill of all faiths *into* the circle of dialogue. It *is* us or them. The question is whether we view others as *them* or as *us*. I vote with God and Isaiah on this one—in an era of separation and divisiveness, where we view most of the world as *them*, we need more "houses of prayer" for "all people" so we can begin to include others in our understanding of the human community as *us*.

> What group in your community or in the world feels most like a *them* that causes anxiety or fear? When have you experienced healing in a relationship where *them* became *us*?

How Does the Bible Shape Our Worship?

A Holy Place

One of the scriptural conversations about worship relates to *place*. We humans need help focusing our attention on God. Abraham marked the places where God appeared or spoke to him, such as Shechem: "So he built there an altar to the LORD, who had appeared to him." The next stop was between Bethel and Ai, where Abraham "built an altar to the LORD and invoked the name of the LORD" (Genesis 12:7-8). Abraham's altar-building is well known in the pages of Genesis, and stories of his altar-building continue outside the Bible. There is an ancient rock in Mecca known as the Ka'ba that has been used by Arabic people as a holy shrine for centuries prior to Muhammad, who helped identify the Ka'ba as an altar by the wandering Abraham.[8] Today, Muslims who make pilgrimages to Mecca prayerfully walk around the Ka'ba, clothed in white to honor the memory of Abraham.

In addition to the various biblical sites that were designated as altars, or holy places, the Israelites built a mobile worship facility called the Tabernacle. The specifications for the Tabernacle are detailed in Exodus 25–27, including the dimensions, the building materials used, and the specific contents. And it all started with an offering—"The LORD said to Moses: Tell the Israelites to take for me an offering; from all whose hearts prompt them to give you shall receive the offering for me. This is the offering that you shall receive from them: gold, silver, and bronze, blue, purple, and crimson yarns and fine linen, goats' hair, tanned rams' skins, fine leather, acacia wood ..." (Exodus 25:1-5).

Later came the permanent Temple, which was built by Solomon, then destroyed by the Babylonians, rebuilt by those who returned from Exile, extensively renovated and expanded by King Herod, and finally destroyed by the Romans. The Temple is the setting for Isaiah's vision of God sitting on a throne amid the seraphs' praise: "In the year that King Uzziah died, I saw the Lord sitting on a throne, high and lofty; and the hem of his robe filled the temple. [One of the] seraphs ... said: 'Holy, holy, holy is the LORD of hosts; the whole earth is full of his glory'" (Isaiah 6:1-3).

Notice how the prophet's vision alternates between the specific time and place. It was the year that King Uzziah died. King Uzziah of Judah was succeeded by Ahaz. Isaiah 7–8 describe Isaiah's mostly unsuccessful attempt to influ-

> Where are the holy places in your life? What makes these places holy for you? Why do you think we need places that are "set apart" for worship?

ence King Ahaz's political policies. So, the vision of God's presence in the Temple is, for Isaiah, a call to political action in a specific time and place of human history.

Note also that when the seraph calls out that "the whole earth is full of his glory," the vision moves from a specific time and place to encompass all of creation (Isaiah 6:3). As we explore some of these Scriptures about worship, we will see the biblical people alternating between specific situations and declarations of God's cosmic and eternal presence. The "hem of his robe" filled the Temple, and his "glory" fills the whole earth (6:1, 3). God, experienced in specific times and places, is not limited to those specific times and places. Because the whole universe is holy, the altar in a given sanctuary is no more holy a space than the closet where the vacuum cleaner is kept. We humans need specific reminders of God's universal presence, so we build altars, we erect tabernacles and temples, we take up offerings for building projects, and we prepare oil for lamps to help us stay focused on God, who is with us at all times and in all places.

The Psalms and Worship

When I was young, the Psalms seemed distant and foreign. It was hard for me to identify with the writers. As I get older, the Psalms seem more relevant, and it is much easier for me to envision the faces of the writers.

The Psalms deal with the entire range of human experience and emotion. That's why they have had such universal application over so many centuries. No expression is "off limits." Pain, a universal human experience, is voiced with graphic clarity: "my bones burn like a furnace" (Psalm 102:3). Yet, praise is like a home base for these writers, one to which they return again and again: "For the LORD is good; his steadfast love endures forever, and his faithfulness to all generations" (100:5).

The Psalms remind us that there are rhythms to life that involve every possible feeling and circumstance—ecstasy, tragedy, victory, defeat, etc. Life, in its particularity and its totality, is reflected in the Psalms against a backdrop of praise: "Worship the LORD with gladness; come into his presence with singing" (100:2).

What is your favorite Psalm? Why? How does the your congregation use Psalms in worship? Read Psalms 100, 102, 134, 145, and 150. How do these psalms connect with worship?

The collection we know as the Psalms was put together with some care. Psalms 120–134 are the "songs of ascents." These songs were sung or chanted by pilgrims as they made their way to Jerusalem. They were marching to Zion, one of the hills of the holy city. Their destination was the Temple: "Lift up your hands to the holy place, and bless the LORD" (134:2).

The Psalms end with a crescendo of praise, beginning with Psalm 145. This psalm is a thoughtful affirmation of God's goodness, for the psalmist writes, "I will extol you, my God and King, and bless your name forever and ever" (145:1). It contains some of the Psalms' great refrains, such as "The LORD is gracious and merciful, slow to anger and abounding in steadfast love. The LORD is good to all, and his compassion is over all that he has made" (145:8-9).

Psalms 146–150 each begin with "Hallelujah!" This is usually translated into English as, "Praise the LORD!" *Hallel* is the Hebrew word for "praise," *u* is an article, like "the," and *jah* (or *yah)* is one of the Hebrew words for "God," as in Yahweh.

Psalm 150, the finale of the collection, is like a symphony of praise, in which the conductor brings in the orchestra sections one at a time to join the chorus of praise—trumpet, lute, harp, tambourine, strings, pipe, and cymbals. Finally, everything in the cosmos is invited to join in this praise chorus: "Let everything that breathes praise the LORD! Praise the LORD!" (150:6).

No one knows for sure who assembled our oldest hymnal, the Psalms. Like our modern hymnal, some of the entries are older than others. Whoever pulled the collection together likely was intentional about the choice of the first psalm, which begins with these words: "Happy are those who do not follow the advice of the wicked, or take the path that sinners tread, or sit in the seat of scoffers; but their delight is in the law of the Lord, and on his law they meditate day and night. They are like trees planted by streams of water" (Psalm 1:1-3a).

The placement of this particular psalm at the beginning of the collection connects the Law with worship. Worship is the natural expression of praise and thanksgiving for one who delights in the Law, whose attitude, priorities and life-direction have been changed by a new orientation. The psalmist sketches a brief outline of this new life and it

> Read Psalm 1. How does it inform your own sense of connection between worship and living daily life God's way?

sets the stage for what follows in the rest of Psalms. It is a way of saying, "This hymnbook belongs to those who are ready to sing a new song and live a new life, a life shaped by the Torah, or Law." The first word of Psalm 1 is "Happy," or "Blessed." Perhaps this is why Jesus' Sermon on the Mount begins with what we call the Beatitudes (Matthew 5:1-12). Jesus may have had Psalm 1 in mind when he began his sermon.

The Law, or Torah, was and is the heart of the Hebrew Bible and faith. Ancient Israelites and modern Jews look to the "Law of Moses" as their most fundamental foundation. When the Bible refers to the "Law," it has in mind the totality of the ethical life. It is life lived under God. It is qualitatively different than life lived at the whim of human nature or desire. In Matthew 5:17-48, Jesus focuses on the inner issues of motive and attitude and the implications, or the outward expressions, of the inner life. Jesus continually points to the impact of the Torah on human relationships.

Notice how Psalm 1 contrasts the two paths: the one who "delights" in the Law vs. the "sinner" or the "wicked." To delight in the Law of the Lord is to have one's basic attitude toward life changed, converted, or repented. The Hebrew people understood that to repent was to change directions.

To choose the path of God's Law, rather than the "path that sinners tread," is to be like a tree "planted by streams of water." It may be difficult for us to appreciate this if we live in an area where streams and water are both abundant. We must keep in mind that these words come out of an arid, desert context. The *wadis* were often underground, visible only by the shrubs that grow on the surface. Flowing streams, like the Jordan River, would look to our eyes like a modest creek, but to biblical eyes, a flowing stream was an enormous resource and treasure. A tree planted there is blessed, or "happy," indeed.

Worship and God's Yearning for the World

Worship is when the faith community presents our life in the world before God to be shaped by God's yearning for our lives and for the world. When Dietrich Bonhoeffer spoke of "religionless Christianity," he may have meant that Christianity is intended to permeate all existence, all of our individual lives, and all of society.[9] The division of life into the sacred and profane is no longer valid. We cannot withdraw religious examination and prophetic questioning from any activity of life. There is no "religious" sphere of life. All of life is lived within God's realm, the sphere of grace. I think Bonhoeffer may have had the prophet Amos in mind, who said, "I hate, I despise your festivals, and I take no delight in your solemn assemblies....

> When have your hopes for the world been lifted through worship? When have you been inspired through worship to engage the world at some point of the world's hurt or need?

But let justice roll down like waters, and righteousness like an ever-flowing stream" (Amos 5:21, 24). Amos is a great biblical connector for us, for he connects devotion to God in worship with our daily life in the world. Such worship unites the journey inward and the journey outward. Out of true worship flows justice, like a mighty water, like an ever-flowing stream.

Worship: Getting Our Act Together

Worship is the way humanity gets its act together. Jesus speaks about worship in the Sermon on the Mount in Matthew: "So when you are offering your gift at the altar, if you remember that your brother or sister has something against you, leave your gift there before the altar and go;

first be reconciled to your brother or sister, and then come and offer your gift" (5:23-24).

Jesus helps us understand the essential and integral connection between worship and human relationships. He is not saying, "Don't attend worship until you get your act together." He is saying, "Worship is the way you get your act together." But, this is not worship *apart from* the sticky issues of daily life. Worship illuminates God's power to transform, redeem, and heal these issues. Jesus doesn't say, "Put your offering back in your pocket and go reconcile yourself with those you have offended." He tells us to *leave* our offering at the altar and then be reconciled.

The altar is the holding place for our offering while we work out our salvation with fear and trembling. The altar is where we transact the divine business of reconciliation with our neighbor. It is the "grace space" where we remind ourselves of God's steadfast love so that our ventures from the altar can become expressions and reflections of God's love in the world.

Worship—Our Opus

So, when we look at ways the Bible shapes our worship, we discover a consistent theme. Worship is our prayerful reflection about the context and content of our daily lives. This reflection is grounded in praise that mysteriously shapes the context and content of our lives. Worship reminds us that we live in the context of gratitude and hope. It helps us see new possibilities. We recognize that God redeems us, which puts us in a posture of readiness to receive, participate in, and work toward the change that God has in mind for the world. We are partners with God in changing the world around us, thus creating a new context for human life. The content of our lives is our *opus*, our work. This means aligning our will, purpose, and yearning with that of God. It means joining our work with God's work of justice and mercy.

> **Closing**
> Sing a favorite hymn of praise.
>
> Silently and prayerfully consider the following questions: When have you gathered your work, your *opus*, thankfully and with praise, as an offering to God? Have you felt yourself consecrated for God's work? Have you found healing, redemption, repentance, and redirection for your life's work through worship? How has worship freed or how might it free you to serve God and others in the world?
>
> Close by praying together the Lord's Prayer.

Notes

[1] *Spirituality for Everyday Living*, by Brian C. Taylor (The Liturgical Press, 1989); pages 30–41.

[2] *Servant Leadership: A Journey Into the Nature of Legitimate Power and Greatness*, by Robert K. Greenleaf (Paulist Press, 1977); page 8.

[3] *Taking the Bible Seriously*, by Leander Keck (Association Press, 1962).

[4] *A New Christianity for a New World: Why Traditional Faith Is Dying and How a New Faith Is Being Born*, by John Shelby Spong (HarperSanFrancisco, 2001); pages 197–200.

[5] For more on St. Anthony, also spelled Antony, see *The Oxford Dictionary of Saints*, by David Hugh Farmer, third edition (Oxford University Press, 1992); pages 25–26. And for more on Anthony as a desert father, see *Freedom of Simplicity*, by Richard Foster (Harper and Row, 1981); pages 56–58 and *Thirsty for God: A Brief History of Christian Spirituality*, by Bradley P. Holt (Augsberg Fortress, 1993); pages 38–40.

[6] *The Oxford Dictionary of Saints*; pages 45–46. Refer also to Note 1 above.

[7] *The Oxford Dictionary of Saints*; pages 133–34, 185–88. For more on the Franciscan and Dominican orders, see *Church History: An Essential Guide*, by Justo L. González (Abingdon, 1996); pages 54–55. And for more on Francis and medieval mysticism, see *A History of the Christian Church*, by Lars P. Qualben (Thomas Nelson and Sons, 1958); page 179.

[8] *God Is One: The Way of Islam*, by R. Marston Speight (Friendship Press, 1989); page 43.

[9] *Prisoner for God: Letters and Papers From Prison*, by Dietrich Bonhoeffer (The Macmillan Company, 1953); page 123.

CHAPTER 7
HOW DOES THE BIBLE
OFFER HELP AND HOPE
FOR CONTEMPORARY LIFE?

Focus: This session will help individuals and communities of faith delve more deeply into the Bible as a source of help and hope for daily living.

Gathering
Sing or read the hymn, "O God, Our Help in Ages Past."

Pray in unison the Prayer of Saint Francis:

Lord, make me an instrument of thy peace;
where there is hatred, let me sow love;
where there is injury, pardon;
where there is doubt, faith;
where there is despair, hope;
where there is darkness, light;
and where there is sadness, joy.

O Divine Master,
grant that I may not so much seek
to be consoled as to console;
to be understood, as to understand;
to be loved, as to love;
for it is in giving that we receive,
it is in pardoning that we are pardoned,
and it is in dying that we are born to eternal life.

The Bible Helps Shape Our View of Time

The Bible presents a linear view of time, beginning with creation and ending with the fulfillment of all things in the "Day of the Lord," in which all injustice will be rectified in a final judgment. The New Testament view of this is that it will be a time when Jesus is recognized as "Lord of lords and King of kings" and when "every knee [will] bend . . . and every tongue [will] confess that Jesus is Lord" (Revelation 17:14; Philippians 2:11).

The daily, weekly, monthly, and yearly rhythms followed by practicing Jews are rooted in the Hebrew Bible. Many of these rhythms are also reflected in the lives of practicing Christians, and Christianity has added some rhythms, such as Christmas, and modified others, such as Pentecost. The Creation story in Genesis 1 speaks of the "evening" and the "morning" of the first day. The Jewish day begins at sundown as one rests in preparation for the day's work.

The seven-day week was etched into the consciousness of the Israelites and the Christian church, by the biblical commandment in Exodus 20:8-11 to remember the sabbath, the seventh day, "and keep it holy." The weekly rhythm of "sabbath" is woven into the spirituality of those who embrace Judaism or Christianity. The Bible also impacts the daily lives of persons who do not think of themselves as "biblical people" or who do not spend much, or any, time reading the Bible. Many people who are thoroughly secular and do not practice a personal "sabbath" benefit from a day off or vacation, both variations of the biblical concept of sabbath.

> Read Exodus 20:8-11. Take a moment to reflect on the pattern of your day, week, month, and year. Create a week in your life, either as a calendar or as a series of drawings. When and where do you intentionally observe "sabbath" in your life?

In America, many of our society's holidays are either grounded in the Bible or adapted to biblical teachings, even though many people may be unaware of their Christian meanings. Halloween is a great example. It was originally a Celtic festival, Samhain (pronounced *sow-in*), that celebrated the new year, the harvest, and return of the spirits of the dead

> How do you celebrate Halloween? All Saints' Day? If you do not currently celebrate All Saints' Day, how might you reclaim it as part of Halloween?

on the eve of the new year. In the seventh century, Pope Boniface IV transformed the celebration into the church's observance of All Saints' Day on November 1 as a day to remember those who have died in the faith.[1] All Saints' Eve, or "All Hallows' Eve," has become a secular, spooky festival that can range from good-natured innocence to a major holiday for practitioners of the occult. The Christian observance of this festival springs from the Bible's affirmation of Jesus' resurrection and the Bible's proclamation that the departed saints are not forgotten but are eternally with God and Christ.

The church year is organized into seasons and celebrations that help us to recall the biblical stories of God's salvation. Exodus 12 describes the festival of Passover, the annual remembrance of the Israelites' liberation from slavery in Egypt. The New Testament proclaims that Jesus' crucifixion and resurrection took place during Passover season. Since Passover was an ongoing, annual Jewish celebration, it was natural for the church to observe an annual celebration

> How do you celebrate Easter? What connections do you see between God's salvation of the people of Israel from slavery in Egypt and God's salvation of all humankind through the resurrection of Jesus Christ?

of Jesus' resurrection during Passover season. Thus it is closely associated with Easter, the day when Christians celebrate the resurrection of Christ. In the early church, a word often used for this Christian celebration is the same as the word for the Passover celebration—*Pasch*.[2]

The early church celebrated the "Great Fifty Days" between Easter and Pentecost. Pentecost, beginning in Acts 2, was a Christian adaptation of the Jewish festival of Pentecost, which came fifty days after Passover. The first known reference to a forty-day season of preparation for Easter comes from the Council of Nicaea in A.D. 325. The word "Lent" comes from an old English term for the spring "lengthening" of days in the Northern Hemisphere. The forty days of Lent do not include Sundays. Forty days, a number that is prominent in the Bible, is used in this context to remember Jesus' 40 days in the wilderness after his baptism. While the Christian seasons of Christmas and Epiphany are not mentioned in the Bible, they commemorate stories that are described in the Bible. Christmas recalls the birth and infancy stories of Jesus as described in Matthew 1–2 and Luke 1–2. Chrysostom made one of the earliest known references to Christmas when he stood before a congregation in Antioch on Christmas Day, A.D. 386, and said, " 'This day ... brought to us, not many years ago, has developed quickly and borne such fruit.' "[3]

Epiphany commemorates God's revelation of Christ. In western traditions of Christianity, it commemorates Christ's revelation to the Gentiles through the magi. In Eastern traditions, it commemorates the baptism of Christ.[4] By the fifth century, a forty-day season of preparation for the Epiphany was being practiced which paralleled Lent and

> How might you reclaim the biblical stories and the opportunities for spiritual growth during the Christian seasons of Advent, Christmas, Epiphany, and Lent?

began about when Advent now begins. Advent, which includes the first four Sundays before Christmas, is a season in which Christians prepare for both the coming of Christ in the birth of Jesus and the second coming of Christ as the Judge at the end of time.[5] Secular customs during the Christmas season often seem to ignore or overlook these biblical origins.

The Bible Helps Us Live With a Sense of Peace

Many persons have found that reading the Bible or Bible-based devotional material to be a helpful morning or evening routine. Countless people regularly gather to read and study the Bible in small groups. Many have been enriched by the practice of keeping a spiritual journal or by writing their reflections after spending some time reading the biblical texts.

> How does engaging the stories of the Bible help you as you learn and grow in faith? How do they help you experience the grace of God through Jesus Christ? When and how do you read or hear the stories in the Bible?

Using these and other methods of engaging the Bible, we find that the stories help us in a number of ways. They give us examples of how God relates to people, as well as how people of faith relate to one another and to the world. They show us examples of those who pray to God and give us instructions about how to pray. They teach us about people of faith who anticipate God's action in human history. Thus, the Bible helps us relate to God and to one another, and it helps us become expectant, hopeful people, confident of God's saving action in our world.

The biblical theme of grace, God's undeserved love, provides many persons with a deep gratitude for life itself. The Bible helps us live our lives by providing an avenue for establishing a saving, life-giving relationship with God, the Creator of the universe we encounter in Scripture. For Christians, this happens through a relationship with Jesus, the person presented by the New Testament as the long-awaited Jewish messiah, or savior. To the extent that one follows Jesus as a disciple, Jesus is "Lord." The Christian faith community uses a variety of words to describe this personal transformation rooted in a relationship with Jesus. Some express it as "being saved," or "receiving salvation." Others speak of being "born again" or "filled with the Holy Spirit." Much of the language we use to describe the life of faith comes from the New Testament. The Bible helps us by giving us a vocabulary and a body of shared stories to express our own faith journey. We find peace that "surpasses all understanding" through Christ who said, "My peace I give to you" (Philippians 4:7; John 14:27).

The Bible Challenges Us

One who spends time with the Bible will find "help in [times of] trouble" (Psalm 46:1). One will also find that the Bible challenges our prevailing attitudes and prejudices and stretches our "comfort zones." One of my heroes is a pastor named John Rutland. He was a prophetic voice for racial harmony in Alabama during the 1950's and 1960's. The Ku Klux Klan once burned a cross in his yard and threatened to harm his family. John was also a tender pastor who cared deeply for those with whom he disagreed politically or socially. He had an amazing capacity both to "comfort the afflicted and afflict the comfortable."

> How has the Bible challenged your "comfort zones"? How does it call you to repentance? How is new life offered through the discomforts of challenge and repentance?

It is tempting to expect the Bible to fit into our own agenda, but the Bible becomes liberating and transformational when we allow our agenda to be shaped by the biblical texts. We sometimes need to ask questions about our interpretations of Scripture: Do we look to the Bible for justification for our attitudes, prejudices, politics, and lifestyles, or do we submit our lives to the authority of the biblical message? Do we see the Bible as an answer book for the questions we have about life, or do we see it as a book that asks us questions about the way we are living our lives?

Serious biblical study is both helpful and humbling. We are helped by the Bible's invitation to an ongoing, honest repentance. This kind of change is sometimes painful but always redemptive. To repent is to turn or turn around. Psychoanalyst Erich Fromm says, "We find in the Bible . . . a marked emphasis on forgiveness, mercy, and on [the human] capacity to 'return.' " The Talmud, a collection of the oral law of the rabbis, uses the term *baal teshuvah* for a repentant sinner, "which means literally 'the master of return.' "[6]

The Bible Helps Us Understand Our Value to God

The biblical stories present God as the intentional Creator of the universe. God values, loves, and has a purpose for humanity and for individuals. The biblical assurance of God's love and forgiveness provides people of faith with a solid foundation for a healthy self-esteem. Many years ago, I attended a youth retreat in which the leader invited the participants to identify themselves as unique and irreplaceable gifts of God. At various points, the youth would say to one another, "You are a unique, irreplaceable gift of God."

Form teams of two or three. Discuss the following questions: How does the Bible help you understand your value to God? How does God's will direct the choices you make from day to day? How do God's purposes for all humans influence your sense of purpose?

The Bible understands humanity, particularly the covenant community of faith, to be in partnership with God, participating in God's mission in the world. Christians sometimes use the phrase "God's will" to describe God's purposefulness or intentionality. In a world experienced by many people to be random and purposeless, the biblical message of God's willfulness helps humans affirm our connections to one another and our individual self-worth. The Bible helps us ask, "What is God's will for the earth?" In light of that broader context, individuals also ask, "What is God's will for my life?"

The Bible helps us make a realistic appraisal of our place in the world. We are extremely important to God, but we are not the center of the universe. God's grace liberates us both from low self-esteem and from self-centeredness. The Bible rejects the human tendency to objectify God. Idols are *objects* and are, therefore, powerless. God is not an object; God is the living Creator of the universe, and therefore sovereign.

The Bible Gives Us a Sense of Community

I heard a new Christian once say to a congregation, "When I gave my life to Jesus, I didn't realize I would get *you* in the bargain!" The Bible not only invites one to be a person of faith but also to become part of a faith community. The Bible invites us to a rhythm of holy solitude and holy engagement with the world. One of the best expressions of a life of prayerful attentiveness is from Brother Lawrence: "The time of business does not with me differ from the time of prayer, and in the noise and clatter of my kitchen, while several persons are at the same time calling for different things, I possess God in as great tranquility as if I were upon my knees at the blessed sacrament."[7]

> How have you or how might you integrate the "time of business" with the "time of prayer"?

As we are drawn into the biblical stories, we are drawn into community. We become children of Abraham. As we live into the New Testament, we become disciples of Jesus. We become part of the Body of Christ. The Bible helps us by giving us a sense of identity. During a 1998 trip to Israel and Egypt, I came to view the six-pointed Star of David not only as a symbol of Judaism, but also a reminder of Jesus, who was born into Judaism and whom I believe to be Messiah. As a reminder of this trip, and as a reminder of my identity, I wear a necklace with a small Star of David that I bought as a souvenir. My wife and I have engraved in our wedding bands the Hebrew words from 1 Kings 3:9, *lebh shomea*, or listening heart. This was inspired by a Roman Catholic priest I met years ago, Kelly Nemick, who was director of the Lebh Shomea House of Prayer. The Bible helps shape our self-understanding and our identity.

> How has the Bible shaped your identity as part of the Christian community? What symbols of our faith have meaning to you? Write a paragraph or create a drawing that illustrates something about your identity as a part of the Christian community.

The Bible helps shape our relationships with others. The Bible calls for us to respect others as we respect God. The Bible invites us to take on the "mind" of Christ, which Philippians 2:5-11 understands to be the mind of a self-giving servant leader. The Bible inspires us to be less controlling and less domineering. The Bible can help us establish appropriate boundaries between ourselves and others. As we develop appropriate and healthy boundaries, we hear the Bible's call to refrain from judging others. In Matthew 7:3-5, Jesus points out the absurdity of pointing out a "speck" in another's eye when there is a "log" in one's own eye. The Bible's assurance that each of us is a person of profound self-worth can help us be less manipulative of others and less emotionally dependent upon others. The Bible can help us muster the strength to resist being manipulated or abused by others. The Bible can help us overcome a victim mentality. The "serenity prayer" adopted by the various Twelve-Step programs has a biblical, psalm-like quality that can help us find a healthy place within our community:

When was a time you stood firmly for the establishment of appropriate emotional or interpersonal boundaries? How might you grow in your efforts to be less manipulative, to resist being manipulated by others, or to overcome the needs to either control others or to see oneself as a victim of others? How do such efforts toward personal growth contribute to the health of the community? How does the Bible help you in these efforts?

"God grant [us] the serenity to accept the things [we] cannot change; Courage to change the things [we] can; and the Wisdom to know the difference."[8]

The biblical call to love one's neighbor provides a goal for a healthier community. The biblical call for justice is one pillar of society's legal system. The biblical call for restraint in seeking revenge makes for a more civil and humane culture. The biblical understanding of God as universal, and not limited to any race or nation, provides a foundation for cooperation with persons of different ethnic or national identities and with those who profess a different faith.

How does the Bible inform your understanding of justice? Of mercy? Of respect for those in other cultural and religious traditions?

How Does the Bible Give Us Hope?

The Hebrew Bible is the holy book for Jews. The combination of the Hebrew Bible (the Christian Old Testament) and the New Testament forms the holy book for Christians. Muslims give priority to the Koran as their holy book, yet some of the Koran is a reflection of the Bible. Many secular people in the western world who do not have a conscious connection to Judaism, Christianity, or Islam benefit, perhaps unknowingly, from the Bible's influence on civility, law, justice, ethics, human rights, and individual freedom.

Some people live out their days with a sense of hopelessness, fatalism, or drudgery. Others live each day with a sense of hope, purpose, and enthusiasm. What makes the difference? For some, it is the drive for economic survival or the prospect of financial reward. For some, it is the sheer fun of one's daily life or the romance of a new relationship, or it could be the excitement of new friendships, a new place of employment, a new residence, or a new possession. But new things and new relationships become old with time. The drive for survival may be overwhelmed by weariness. Even the allure of financial wealth can become dull through boredom, soured relationships, or failing health.

Some people are able to withstand incredible adversity when the storms of life are raging. Their attitude toward life is not dependent on external factors, such as weather, the actions of other people, political stability, or financial security. With courage, confidence, and creativity, they face the process of aging or declining health. How are they able to do this?

Some people are thoughtful, caring, and loving. They consistently think of others first. They willingly sacrifice for others or serve others. They work for the common good. They encourage others. They live with a sense of hope. How are these people able to get beyond themselves and their own needs?

The Bible is grounded in the belief that the universe is neither random nor accidental. A loving Creator has created the cosmos with purpose and intentionality. This Creator of the universe loves and values all persons yet selects, or "calls," some persons and groups through a sense of mission or of being "chosen," not for privilege or status, but for service to the world.

The characters and stories of the Bible can help us live with hope, purpose, and enthusiasm. Abraham can be a model of hope that does not allow age to limit one's goals or one's willingness to learn, grow, and initiate new endeavors. Abraham can be a model of how to live peacefully and respectfully in an alien culture. Abraham is the spiritual ancestor of Judaism, Christianity, and Islam. The biblical stories of Abraham can provide healing for today's troubled world through the creation of common vocabulary and through common themes of hope, purpose, and enthusiasm that are contained in the traditions surrounding Abraham.

Every human life and every human community needs a balance of freedom and responsibility. Lives and communities are wounded when persons act with selfish license and disregard for others—when freedom is abused in the name of personal satisfaction. Lives and communities are injured when persons act with tyranny or oppressiveness by creating laws or systems that unfairly restrict human life and stifle the human spirit. Individual humans sometimes place repressive laws or rules upon themselves, inflicting self-destructiveness or creating low self-esteem that robs a person of hope, purpose, or enthusiasm. The stories of Moses can help us find an energizing balance for our lives and our world as we exercise the twin gifts of freedom and responsibility.

Human communities need strong leadership, good governance, and fair systems of justice. They need high idealism, sound ethics, and dependable integrity—all components of what the Bible calls "righteousness." The Bible can help us develop an ethic for our common humanity in a world of many religions and value systems. The Bible places great hope and trust in human leaders, as in the hope for a leader like King David. The Bible also recognizes that the voice of God and the voice of the people must sometimes be raised *over* and *against* those in leadership, and so we have the enormous gift of the prophetic tradition—such as prophets like Nathan, Elijah, Amos, and Jeremiah.

The Bible points us to the future with the confidence that God transcends time and is ultimately in charge of the future. Christian hope dwells in the person of Jesus. The cornerstone of Christian hope is our belief that Christ has been raised from death—that we are invited to participate in resurrection and eternal life. We can be energized with hope that defies all obstacles and cannot be defeated. We can be confident that there is purpose and meaning in the future. And we can face each day with gratitude and enthusiasm, for we have been given the precious gift of life and a foretaste of life eternal. One of my mentors was a pastor named Claude Whitehead. He lived life with confidence that God was using him to help others experience a deeper spiritual life. Claude believed the basis for evangelism in the early church was the contagious spontaneity of 1 Peter 3:15, which he translated: Always be prepared to give an account for the *hope* that is within you.

We can begin each day with the awareness that we are beneficiaries of a blessing, promised to all humanity through Abraham (Genesis 12:2-3), that we can live with a sense of newness, power, and a relationship with our Creator (Jeremiah 31:31-34). We can greet each new day with the anticipation of God's action in our lives and in our world (Joel 2:28-29).

We can begin our day with the hope of peace on earth (Isaiah 2:2-4; Luke 2:14). And we can greet each sunset and each sunrise by joining with the psalmist and with persons from all times and places who are already singing: "This is the day that the LORD has made; let us rejoice and be glad in it" (Psalm 118:24).

Closing Worship
Read or sing the first two verses of "My Hope Is Built on Nothing Less."

Pray together this prayer, inspired both by Revelation 22:1-2 and "A Statement of Faith of the United Church of Canada":

Almighty God, when we face the barren places of life, remind us of the river of the water of life that flows from you and from our Christ. When we face questions we cannot answer or issues we cannot resolve, remind us of the tree of life and your limitless bounty. When we face the fear of brokenness or violence, remind us that within the leaves of your tree of life is the aloe of Christ, which is for the healing of the nations. When we face our own mortality and the fleeting temporality of planet earth, remind us that Jesus is our judge and our hope and that in life, in death, in life beyond death, you are with us. We are not alone. Thanks be to God. Amen.[9]

Notes

[1] For more details about the origins of Halloween and All Saints' Day, see "The History of Halloween," on the History Channel's website at: http://www.historychannel.com/exhibits/halloween/?page=origins.

[2] See "Pasch" in *The Oxford Dictionary of the Christian Church*, second edition, edited by E.L. Cross and E.A. Livingstone (Oxford University Press, 1983); page 1036.

[3] To read more about the Christian year, see the sixth volume in the Supplemental Worship Resource series, *Seasons of the Gospel: Resources for the Christian Year* (Abingdon, 1979); page 22.

[4] See "Epiphany" in *The Oxford Dictionary of the Christian Church*; page 465.

[5] See "Advent" in *The Oxford Dictionary of the Christian Church*; page 19.

[6] See *You Shall Be As Gods: A Radical Interpretation of the Old Testament and Its Tradition*, by Erich Fromm (Fawcett Premier Books, 1966); page 133.

[7] *The Practice of the Presence of God*, by Brother Lawrence (Fleming H. Revell Company, 1958); page 8.

[8] For more, see the devotional for February 13 in *Letting God: Christian Meditations for Recovering Persons*, by A. Philip Parham (HarperSanFrancisco, 1987).

[9] To read the "Statement of Faith of the United Church of Canada," see *The United Methodist Hymnal* (883).